**Why the most authentic
brands succeed.**

Second Edition Revised 2017 & Reprinted 2019.

Edited by Tony Ingram.

Printed in USA.

For more information, please contact buildgreatbrands@jcinquina.com.

Cover Concept by Quim Marin Studio, Barcelona.

Build
Great
Brands

Why the most authentic
brands succeed.

John Cinquina
Revised Edition

Contents

**Build
Great
Brands**

Chapter 1

An introduction

Executive Summary

In the beginning was the brand.

In this chapter we lay the foundation for the entire book by exploring its reason for existence, the key topics contained within and the value promise when the content is practically applied to your organization's brand.

1.1 Start with a story

I share a love/hate relationship with flying. I have flown with the same airline consistently for a number of years now but recently I've considered moving across to a different carrier. Why? You may ask. Well a number of friends and colleagues have made the switch and are completely in love with Virgin. I haven't looked at prices. I'm not aware of their points program and Virgin certainly hasn't contacted me as a prospect. Still, my friends insist that I should give this new carrier a go.

As I sit down for coffee one afternoon with one of these friends, the conversation starts up again. "It's just everything", he shouts as if I'm on the other side of the room. (Why do people do this when they're excited?) He can hardly contain his passion. "The experience is incredible. The check-in is easy. Nothing is too much effort for them. I love their uniforms. The planes look like discos. The introductory video is amazing. They take care of me. Their menus are so inspiring and I think Richard has done an exceptional job." So now you're on a first name basis with Branson?

My friend's experience has culminated in a belief that Virgin and Richard Branson is an exceptional airline brand to fly with. Did it run on time? Well he didn't say. Did he eat the food? To be honest, I wouldn't know. What is the safety record of Virgin? I never asked. But here I am being arm-wrestled to at least trial this new brand. And why? There's no commission structure motivating him to refer me. Just complete brand loyalty.

Interestingly enough, I'm not even that dissatisfied with my current carrier. I've never had any complaints with them. But most importantly, and I mean MOST importantly, I am not as satisfied with my airline as he is with his. I'm the guy on the other side of the fence wondering what it's like to graze in the other paddock.

The story demonstrates why I believe in the power of great brands. I believe that when you truly connect with your audience and 'wow' them with a brand experience that they talk about, as my friend did to me, than you're onto something with the potential to grow exponentially.

"I believe in the power of great brands"

When we look at the story of Virgin, there has been no dumb luck involved with this success story and my friend's loyalty is the outcome of an investment into brand. Virgin fought for its position in the airline industry from the beginning and subsequently, it became known as the challenger brand. As a challenger, they drew from an 'anti-establishment' narrative, encouraging customers to come and try something new. For Virgin to say they were different and new was one thing but they had to follow through and herein they found a brand promise that has carried them till today. From that promise of 'different', innovation was birthed and Virgin focused on injecting brand personality into every point of the brand experience. Regardless of performance, even today, when you experience 'Virgin' the brand, it is a different experience in comparison to the more conservative carriers. Virgin has found its brand position in the market and it stands for something.

1.2 Build Great Brands: the book

We live in a world with an ever increasing array of choice. Time and time again I have seen that, even in over-saturated markets, there are always brands that have found a way to engage and connect with their market and to differentiate themselves from the others, while others fail to survive. In these instances it usually doesn't matter how many competitors continue to enter their space, because these companies have found the right formula to capture their market and grow.

So how do you become one of these winning companies instead of one that struggles to find leads and customers? How do you continue to grow in a market that becomes saturated with competitors? How do you let potential customers know that you are better and in materially relevant ways? How do you keep them close and develop a loyal customer base?

These are the questions that plague all those in charge of driving business growth and it's the reason I have written this book.

'Build Great Brands' echoes my passion and belief that all businesses and organizations, given the will and the support, can grow great brands. I have seen it happen and continue to see it happen.

This book is short and concise and I have worked hard to keep it that way. It's not designed to be placed on your 'books to read (one day)' list. Let's face it, we've all got that list and it keeps growing. Instead, this book is a 'right now' book with strategies and actions for your current business and brand situation.

Your brand stands for something: it stands for you. It impacts and influences how your audience perceives you and hence your ability to grow your business. Your decision to invest into it is an important one. We will focus on the importance of brand building and provide you with practical aids to build your very own great brand.

For too long brand has been perceived as 'nice to have' rather than 'need to have'. This perception has led many organizations to believe that brand is mostly about aesthetic, touchy feely stuff and not really linked to business growth. For that reason, they don't devote resources to it. Fixing the IT system may be worth spending money on, but solidifying their brand position is not.

"All businesses and organizations, given the will and the support, can grow great brands"

For whatever reason, no one has convincingly shown these companies the link between business growth and branding. My hope is that this perception is about to change. "Build Great Brands" doesn't dance around the topic. It goes straight to the key issue of how branding can be a waste of time and money and how best to avoid that from happening. The book dives into the correlation between strategic growth, brand and sales. In doing so I will lay the groundwork to help you recognize and grab hold of business growth opportunities that exist right now for you and your brand.

BUILD GREAT BRANDS, THE BOOK

WHAT IS BRAND?

WHY IS IT IMPORTANT?

HOW BRAND CORRELATES TO GROWTH

HOW TO USE BRAND MORE EFFECTIVELY

PRACTICAL STEPS

IMPLEMENT WHAT YOU'VE LEARNED INTO YOUR BUSINESS

1.3 It can't happen overnight

One hour with a notepad and a coffee is not enough to articulate your understanding of your business. Defining your brand is a journey that forces you to ask hard questions. You know...the ones you gloss over because they're a bit too deep to spend any great amount of time on? As business owners, business development managers or marketing managers, we are responsible for driving business growth. As a result, we get used to working hard. In fact, very hard. In this 'working hard', we can risk getting caught up in reactive activity as a measure of success - working in our business rather than on our business, as the saying goes. Tasks driving tasks driving tasks but not necessarily obtaining results. "Never mistake motion for action," is how Hemingway put it.

But if you want to build your brand, and that is hopefully why you are reading this book, then you must learn to 'delete, delegate or delay' your other work, at least for a time. For now, the most important thing is to direct your attention and head-space towards the drivers that will grow your business. Brand is most certainly one of those drivers.

"Defining your brand is a journey that forces you to ask hard questions."

1.4 Insights and secrets

Whether you are an entrepreneur, a business owner who's been doing this a while, or a manager, this book is written for you. Everything I think will help you understand the foundations of brand and achieve growth is here. The content of this book is derived directly from my work with people in your exact positions. It contains theory, practical applications and take home exercises that you can use today to build your brand.

I am, among many things, a passionate student of brand building and I am confident that great branding can help change our world and the worlds of the businesses that use this information effectively. For this reason, my greatest hope is that you will discover and learn something in this book that brings about a positive result for you today.

You are more than welcome to email me if you have any questions John@jcinquina.com.

And now, let's commence the journey. Good luck.

1.0 Introduction

Build
Great
Brands

Chapter2

So what is a brand anyway?

Executive Summary

Let's lay the foundation.

This chapter helps lay the framework for the language and definitions used within the book. It looks at the basis of brand, what a brand contains and how we collectively define brand as a word and a practise. Most importantly, this chapter explores the foundations of why brand is so important to any great business.

2.1 Defining brand

Let's go back to the very beginning and ask the question, what is brand? "Isn't it just a logo?" I hear some of you ask. If this is what comes to mind it's time to shut your front door and put the phone on silent because this book has just became the single most important guide that you will ever read.

Firstly, brand is much more than just a logo. It is the entire experience that your potential and existing customers will have of your company, your product and your service. It encompasses everything you stand for. The key to understanding the power of brand is to consider that brand is not just about communicating what you do, but communicating who you are and why you do what you do. It may be surprising to learn that most consumers actually engage far more with the latter and because of this, the 'why' behind the 'what' is vastly more important.

The word 'brand' itself was invented to describe a mark. It is derived from the old Norse word 'brandr,' meaning 'to burn' and was used by livestock owners to brand their animals and identify them. The brand was there for life and very clearly helped people identify who the animal belonged to. In that regard, I suppose you could say the first brands were very effective. Even today, whether you like it or not, the idea of 'brandr' is still sound because your brand defines you, and whilst it may not need to be with your business for life, it does takes time to change it.

As commerce and business developed into the nineteenth century, the term brand became a popular metaphor for a recognisable symbol of ownership. It is this recognisable mark that defines your organization to the consumer and in a lot of cases it may be the only way they know it's you. For example, how do you know a McDonald's franchise is close? The golden arches peeking out from behind the traffic on the highway. Those golden arches are the bedrock of their brand.

When done well, a brand should conjure up all the meaning, messaging, values and statements that your organization stands for. Take a look at the following brand symbols (what I call 'icons' or logos of the brand) and consider the emotions and perceptions that come to mind:

  Quality, prestige, status

  Performance, competitiveness

  Fast, reliable, affordable

  Fun, innovators, elegant

  Business, functional, legacy

Even when similar, icons can emote very different things and this is the impact of well-differentiated branding awareness.

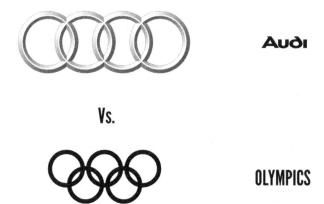

Vs.

OLYMPICS

A brand's emotion or meaning does not define its function, however, because brand is not about engagement more than recognition. In fact, its three primary functions (what it achieves) can be defined as:

1. Choice: Brands help consumers choose from an array of options available to them.

2. Reassurance: Brands reassure customers that they have made or are about to make, the right choice by communicating the value, quality and expectations that the product or service brings. The communication reinforces and aligns with a customer's expectations for that brand.

3. Identify and remember: The distinctive colors, imagery, icons and messaging of a brand distinguish it from others and help consumers identify it for future recognition and is the beginning of loyalty.

2.2 What does a brand contain?

Over the years brand has been misrepresented and overused as a word, not just in the marketing industry but throughout business and has therefore lost a great deal of its meaning and power. It's important that we establish that it is not merely the process of designing a logo. At its core, brand has and always should be a discipline, a creative craft and scientific process. It is used to build awareness and develop loyalty. When a company offers to design your logo, they are not creating a brand for you. The logo is important but it is really just the tip of the iceberg. There is a lot that happens under the surface of equal or greater importance before that logo even comes into existence. Without engaging that activity, brands can appear 'vanilla' and meaningless. This is perhaps the worst, and least effective kind of brand · one that stands for nothing. The quality of design though important is not what defines your brand. It is the substance underneath that leads to a quality outcome.

THE EXTERNAL - LOGO

The Things We See
Logo
The brand elements
Brand collateral pieces
Point of sales templates
Ad campaigns
Sales documentation
Targeted messaging and slogans
Content and copywriting

The Things We Don't See

Audience research & engagement
Core purpose (why are we here?)
Company direction (where are we going?)
Brand values
Value proposition to audience
Brand promises and commitments
Communications framework
Creative ideation
Organisational wide buy-in
Internal messaging
Language tone of voice

THE INTERNAL CONVERSATION

2.3 Getting your business direction right first

Before that earth shattering logo can be born, a lot of internal dialogue needs to happen. Whether you're a start-up or mature organization in need of a re-brand, this process remains the same and it starts with clearly articulating your business direction.

As we have seen, great brands articulate who you are, where you're going and why you do what you do. Also, great brands start with a logo but require more to communicate the depth of the message. In order for this to happen, you yourself have to understand these things. You can never underestimate the power of this understanding when it comes to branding your organization to the market.

The standard one page logo questionnaire is great for designing a logo but not for articulating a brand. That questionnaire will no doubt focus on what you do but the 'what' is always secondary to the 'why'. Understanding the 'why' will help you decide what your brand will become. Here's what the process looks like.

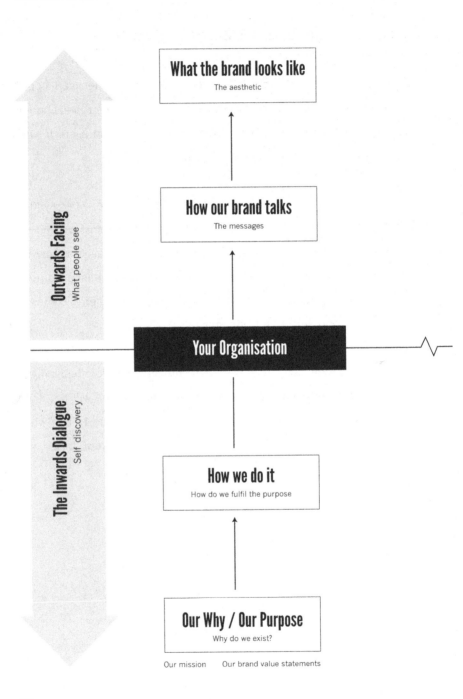

It starts with looking at your business as a whole and starting with your WHY or your PURPOSE. From there, the WHAT needs to connect with the WHY.

When you know your WHY, you can articulate your PURPOSE. Why you do what you do should be the primary driver for developing a core purpose statement (the reason your business exists).

When you can articulate your PURPOSE, you can define HOW you intend to fulfil that purpose.

Only then do you realizewhether WHAT you're doing is actually WHAT you should be doing and often tweaking that is key to ensuring your business is the fulfilment of what you want it to be.

When you know the WHAT and you understand the connection that it has with your WHY, then we've got a diagram (like the one left of page) and this is a key part of the branding process. It's an incredible foundation for your brand.

A consistent and strategically focused brand leads to a stronger and more consistent brand image that engages and connects with your audience. That connection to your audience is what often leads to new business and re-acquisition of current business but the inwards facing dialogue is where it all begins.

If someone just wants a logo, business card and website, then it's not building a brand because what's missing is this very important part of the process; strategy. It may be designing some nice looking visual elements. They may look great and the investment of time may be less, but the process and hence the outcome will be second-rate, and subsequently, the brand will under-perform in its ability to help an organization achieve goals.

2.4 The process

The process of brand is a series of unending questions. We can never really run out of questions. The more we know, the more clearly we can articulate our brand. So we continue to ask questions, to conduct research, to ask more questions, to design, to ask more questions, to consult, and you guessed it, to ask more questions. This commitment to questioning will enable your brand to become an evolving organism, flexible and agile enough to change and pivot as your business grows. It also helps you gain clarity on direction, personality and values. Often we bang these out in a two hour workshop and never look at them again, but constant question asking forces us to dig deeper in order to challenge and refine. This gets us to a point where we can punch our fist in the air and stand behind every statement that is said. That's when you know a brand is in the works. If you're after a stage-by-stage look at what the brand process looks like, see the next diagram.

Step 1 ·······························►

| Articulating our goals and defining our needs | Understanding who we are, why we exist and where we are going |

Step 2 ·······························►

| Defining our core messages | Developing targeted messages | Creating a visual style that defines the look and feel |

Step 3 ·······························►

| Designing the logo identity elements | Rolling the identity out across all the touch points between your organisation and its audience (i.e. print, web, video etc...) |

2.5 The first step

It's in the first step that we find our launch pad. Without it, the rest suffers. As I've mentioned, it's in this understanding of who you are and what you're trying to achieve · your core messages · that you find the foundation for brand. There are a series of key questions to ask yourself in this process.

What are our goals?
1. What are we trying to achieve in our business?
2. What are the goals of a branding audit? What do we hope to achieve?
3. How do we intend to reach our goals?
4. What does our potential and existing customer experience look like?
5. What do we need in a brand (practical items)? (This is a conversation that is best had with an agency)

Who am I?
1. Who are we and how would we define ourselves?
2. What is our culture? What statements describe us best?
3. What is our purpose, why do we exist as an organization?

Who is my audience?
1. Who is my audience? Who are they really?
2. What do they want? Is that just an assumption? What do they really want?
3. What motivations drive them to those wants?
4. What benefit beyond transactional do our customers get from engaging with us?

5. What emotional benefit do they receive?

6. What are their frustrations? Their worries? Their fears? How do we help?

7. Is there a primary problem that we're solving? What is it?

Our customers

8. Do our customers understand us?

9. Why did they choose us? Why do they continue to choose us? (Ask them if you don't know)

2.6 The gap

In just a few questions, we have already gathered a great deal of the knowledge required to help bridge the gap between US (the company) and THEM (the audience). The more we know about both parties, the easier it will be to bridge the gap.

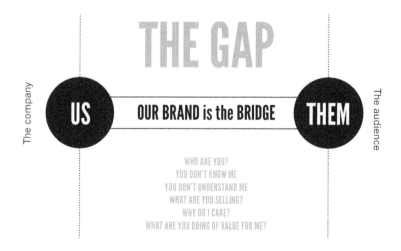

THE GAP

The company | US | OUR BRAND is the BRIDGE | THEM | The audience

WHO ARE YOU?
YOU DON'T KNOW ME
YOU DON'T UNDERSTAND ME
WHAT ARE YOU SELLING?
WHY DO I CARE?
WHAT ARE YOU DOING OF VALUE FOR ME?

Think of your brand as the opening negotiator for you. The guy you send in to break the ice and warm up the crowd. Your brand can get a lot done in the initial stages of somebody's experience with your company and it all happens before you enter the room. It can make the sales process easier or harder – it's completely up to you and how dedicated you are to working on bridging the gap early.

Who we are, why we exist and what we do should connect with the needs and wants of our audience. We leverage the knowledge of our customers to help create that bridge. We mould our offering, we structure our value proposition and we prepare our creative all to reinforce that connection. The intentionality of the brand is not lost because the results are realized the moment you walk into the room with your potential customer or the moment they walk into the store to see your product. Whatever the sales engagement process, our brand does the legwork in building expectations, defining need and connecting with the customer we're trying to win over. By letting your brand do the initial hard work, you put yourself in a better position.

2.7 You are not your market

"Brand is not what you say it is. It's what **they** say it is"
· Marty Neumeier

Brand is the consistency of opinion on 'who' your organization is. Your brand is not what you think it is. It can't be.
In fact, your opinion of the brand holds very little relevance. It's

sometimes a tough conversation to tackle with people who have been embedded in the organization as owners or business drivers for some time. Reason being, there is an immense amount of emotional attachment tied up in your opinion of your business.

You are biased, let's face it, and so you should be. You should think that your product or service is the best thing that ever hit the market. There's no shame in admitting that and it's that belief that will enable you to succeed, so don't ever let go of it.

But your brand is not for you and it certainly isn't measured by you. "They" are the ones that measure it and what "they" think is the real sum of your brand effectiveness. It makes sense then to understand how "they" measure it.

By now, no doubt you realizethat they are the community, the public, the audience, the prospects. Interestingly enough, there's a formula for how they measure you.

EXPERIENCE A + EXPERIENCE B + EXPERIENCE C....
= Brand Perception

As my friend's perception of Virgin was calculated, so it is with your brand. It is in the experiences that someone has with your brand that will determine the overall perception.

When you think about it, this makes sense really. Perception can only be defined by experience. These experiences can take on many different forms. It may be the first visit to your website, or the phone call they make, or the auto responder from their enquiry form. It may be the meeting you have with them, or the first invoice that comes through after they approve the service. It could even be the follow up call you make six months later or the post project hamper you send. It might be the first advert they see on television or the newspaper article written about your company. No matter what these experiences are, they work together as a sum to provide a positive, indifferent or negative perception of your brand. It's the positive or negative perception that a person is left with after engaging with you once, twice or a hundred times and it's vitally important in your ability to convert, to retain and to receive referrals.

"Perception can only be defined by experience"

2.8 Customer experience diagram

I encourage every company starting down the path of a brand process to draw a customer experience diagram that maps out all the experiences a customer will have with your organization across every single stage. This understanding helps us map out the touch points and opportunities that we have to help create positive experiences that a customer has with us.

This may start from the moment they walk in the door and you can be as detailed as you want. I don't think there's a point that I've ever said "too much detail" because every single interaction counts.

Those interactions are what makes up your brand from logos, brochures, your office, sales material, website, app, video, social media presence, thank you cards and even the way the phone is answered. I'm sure you get the idea but they are tangible interactions that a customer can see, feel and touch.

Once we know what those potential interactions are, we get to work on making them better. In this collective effort to effectively brainstorm better ways of improving our customers' brand experiences, we find that their experiences improve. We know from our formula that if we improve that experience, hey presto, we're building brand perception. We'll explore later on just how this impacts sales.

Here's a list of potential touch-points to include in your customer experience map and later on we'll go deeper into what that customer experience map looks like.

Brand Experience Touchpoints

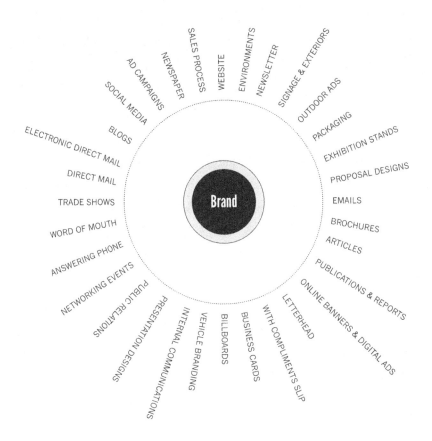

2.9 The choice to be great

Great businesses have great brands. The two go hand in hand.

For those of us trying to build great businesses (hopefully all of us reading this book), it's vital that our brand reflects this greatness because good enough is no longer good enough. We exist in an age facing the end of average. Your product and service may be world class and your intention may be to build the kind of company that your customers love contributing to, as my friend did for Virgin, but until you find a way to communicate that to your audience in a way that is compelling, the opportunity to win them over may be lost. The same goes for potential employees. Online job boards report that in scenarios comparing two similar companies with similar ads, the company with the superior brand received more applications (by a long way).

The companies that are great choose to invest into great branding because of this core belief that it should never and can never be left behind as they push forward. Great brand development must accompany this quest for greatness.

"Great businesses have great brands. The two go hand in hand."

2.10 How to measure success

So with that in mind, we must articulate what great success looks like. Unless we can measure brand performance, we can never really understand whether it's achieved its objectives or not.

"It looks pretty" can't be the only measuring tool for the success of a brand project. You're making the agency's job too easy if this is the case. There are a lot of people good at making things look pretty but a brand must align with the business' primary objectives and goals.

No matter what industry you're in, or channel you market through, or audience you target, brand is universal in its ability to help achieve success for an organization. That success can be defined differently but aligning the goal of a brand with the goals of an organization should be the first thing we do before we even start. Note that the order is important. The goals come first. The brand is there to serve the purpose of the organization's definition of success. Success for a company is always forward looking and so the brand must help move the company forward to that defined "success" point that will be the measure of its success. Therefore, in evaluating where we go as a brand, the first question must always be:

What are you trying to achieve in your organization? What is your goal?

...And from there, we can then move to an equally important

second question.

How can your brand help you achieve this goal, quantitatively and qualitatively?

...Thirdly.
How will we measure the ability of this brand in achieving our goals?

Don't be fooled – these aren't supposed to be easy questions but they are worth really spending some time articulating answers for.

2.11 All the parts combine to work together

The logo is not everything but it's a part of the mechanism of brand and these parts within the mechanism work together to ensure you have a well-oiled machine. A great logo is not enough.

Remove the Mercedes logo from a Mercedes car and you will still know it's a Mercedes. Take the Apple logo off an Apple laptop and you will still know it's an Apple. Take the Apple logo off Apple branding and you will still recognize the poster or the ad because the brand has worked hard to build a visual style and tone of messaging that we recognize even if the logo is not present.

Additionally, you know when you're in an Apple store or when buying a Mercedes car – the experience is certainly something to write home about.

Brand then, is the combination of a number of visual devices and experiences designed to communicate a message, a message that doesn't end at the first interaction. The story develops as you continue to interact with the brand and in that consistency you are able to form that positive perception. In fact, the longer a consumer interacts with a brand that is consistent in message, in tone and in aesthetic, the more in line the beliefs the consumer has will be with who you really are.

2.12 Good and Different

That perception is #1 for you as you continue to build a great brand. Within competitive landscapes, we are trying to achieve two things. An audience perception that considers us both GOOD

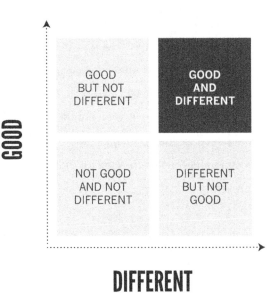

and DIFFERENT.

You may already be good and different.

You may know that.

The question is, does your audience know that?

If they don't, how do we create a brand experience that enables them to form that perception?

Good and different sells brands. Good attracts consumers to what we're selling and different differentiates us from the other brands competing for their attention.

"The primary focus of your brand message must be on how special you are, not how cheap you are. The goal must be to sell the distinctive quality of the brand."

- Kerry Light

**Build
Great
Brands**

Chapter 3

Know who you're speaking to

Executive Summary

Your audience is everything.

Without understanding your audience, your brand cannot be effective. This chapter shows why your target market is so important and how to win them over by understanding their needs, wants and frustrations.

3.1 No, it's not everyone

Know who you're speaking to as a brand... and no, it's not everyone.

It's not even everyone aged 15-45. Be more specific.

Why are people so scared of being more specific?

It's as if we're fearful that we'll miss out on business. But it's exactly the opposite.

As we narrow our focus, our effectiveness increases.

So be as specific as you can.

John Russell, the president of Harley-Davidson, said, "the more you engage with customers, the clearer things become and the easier it is to determine what you should be doing." Which is exactly what Harley -Davidson did.

3.2 Just ask

One of the scariest things we can do in business is to ask customers for their opinion. We get so fearful of what they may say, and of how much work will result once we discover how wrong we are. So sometimes we decide not to ask. I know it sounds silly when put like that, but that is how we sometimes think. It is, of course, precisely the wrong strategy. When you engage with your customer group, it fosters their loyalty and brand ownership, as they feel included (in your plans to make the company better).

Imagine you've been asked to give a presentation on a topic that you know well. The presentation is to a crowd of one hundred people. It's a significant size and they are all eager to hear what you have to say. Imagine yourself preparing for it.

What would you say?

How would you structure your talk?

Would you use slides, visual devices, videos, diagrams, handouts or all of these?

How would you ensure you got your message across effectively?

Now imagine that group of people is a grade 3 class of children.

No doubt your entire tact changes.

What you say, how you say it, what you use as supporting evidence and how much you say all changes with that single variable: your audience.

Imagine this talk is going to be televised. Here it is the medium and not the audience that changes. But once again the alteration of a single variable changes your content, your delivery and your method of preparation.

"One of the scariest things we can do in business is to ask customers for their opinion."

It's much the same with brand.

The trap we fall into as business drivers is the assumption that our audience wants to hear what we want to tell them. I wish it were the case, but it's just not.

I liken it to a husband buying his wife for her birthday the power tool he's hankered after or giving his six-year old daughter the latest business growth publication, expecting that she'll love it. She just wanted a bike with streamers. We don't do this of course, because we know our families so well. We know what they want and what will make them happy. We need to do the same for our clients. Instead of taking the time to understand them, understand their needs and give them what they value, we tend to give them what we want. It may be that we're scared of asking. It may be that we think we're the audience. It may just be that we never thought to ask the question.

Therein lies our first hard truth in branding: You are not your customer. Even if you are your customer, you're not! Your taste probably doesn't matter. Your opinion on color isn't valid. Your design aesthetic and idea on what people want is likely skewed. The key selling points in your mind are not necessarily important. They may be valuable for the process but they are not the be all and end all.

The beautiful thing about having our audience tell us what they want is that we can literally re-word what they've asked for and serve it up to them on a silver platter. They help us sell to them.

The second hard truth: Your neighbor is not your audience (even if they are). We should not be so quick to get their opinion. (And by 'neighbor' I mean anyone who is not your potential customer.). In fact, we should be carefully selective about whose opinion we seek, because everyone will have something to say.

"So I took this over to Bill's house, and Bill thinks...." is a sentence that strikes fear into my veins. I would like Bill. In fact, I'd probably love Bill and can't wait to go to his house for a BBQ next weekend. He has some great ideas, but it's unlikely he fits the profile of our target market and its unlikely he has the level of understanding that you've built a great deal of time building as a foundation for the creative design process. For those reasons (and more) we don't want Bill making the decision on what will impact the performance of the business for years to come.

"You are not your customer"

3.3 Strategic from the outset

You can't just fluke your way to a great brand. Very few companies have ever survived and thrived without a strategic focus on how they brand. Those that have form the very small group that I call "annoying exceptions" and that group (who often possess government policy driven monopolies) I'd like to ignore because for the 99.99% of us who that won't happen to, it just hurts our feelings.

Even for the business that continues to thrive without an investment into brand, there are identifiable missed opportunities. These companies are experiencing brand performance issues because they're not taking full advantage of the opportunities available to them. Brand may contain great design but it doesn't start there. We must consider how our design, our messaging and our value offering engages with the audience alongside how it speaks to their needs, their designs and their frustrations.

In doing this, we must also ensure it is compelling and to do this, a brand must perform two key tasks:
1. Understand its audience
2. Deliver a compelling value offering, both in message and in creative.

It is its ability to be compelling that separates a great brand from all the other brands.

A compelling brand draws people in.
It masters the sales challenge of addressing their needs, desires, frustrations and wants with a compelling solution. It becomes the difference between consumers saying yes or saying no to what you are offering.

Bottom line. Your brand must firstly understand the audience and secondly develop a message that engages with that audience. Trust me when I say that the return on investment will make this exercise more than worthwhile. This is why the biggest companies in the world invest into understanding their audience and creating a compelling brand to engage with them. T. Michael Glenn of Fedex says "Managing a brand is a lot like shaving...if you do it every day, you look pretty good. If you miss a couple of days, you start to look a little scruffy."

"A compelling brand draws people in"

3.4 Understand the problem

So what does it mean to understand our audience? Knowing their age and their general demographic information is a start, but it is still quite one-dimensional. Remember, we're trying to narrow our focus in order to increase the impact of our message. We need to go deeper.

We must know what their problem is and how we are solving it.
At the heart of every value offering is the ability to solve a problem or meet a need, and to understand what you're really selling. A hint is that it is ALWAYS more than what we think. It always goes deeper.

Here are some questions to begin with:
1.   Who is my current customer?
2.   Who is my ideal customer?
3.   Are they the same, or different? Why?
4.   What are their habits?

5.   What cars do they want to drive?

6.   What shows do they watch on television?

7.   What do they spend their money on?

8.   What are their aspirations and dreams?

3.5 The two levels of needs

Until we determine what the needs of our audience really are, we can never develop a brand that connects with them. There are two levels of need to consider. Surface level and then a deeper, more emotional level. These can almost always be linked but the real value of your brand connection is created at the deeper level we refer to.

1. Surface needs: To eat, to drink, to sleep, to be comfortable, to be pain free, to be clothed.

Example: You need to eat. Eat at my restaurant. Eat great food at my restaurant. These can be considered surface selling points because they speak to surface needs.

2. Emotional needs: To be loved, accepted, to feel good about yourself, to feel like a good person, to be praised, to receive reward and recognition for your work, to be thanked, to be accepted.

Example: The experience of a meal with the people you love at my establishment. The privilege of having us cook a meal for your family. Experiencing something with your family that makes them feel special These are deeper (tier two) needs and connect with stronger motivations. Connecting with this level will produce a greater level of engagement.

For instance, a medical practitioner may see her job as helping relieve pain. Being pain free is the surface need for the patient. But when we engage deeper we discover that it is what being pain free allows the patient to enjoy that unlocks our branding direction. Spending more time with her kids, feeling like a great parent, living a longer life with the ones she loves. The "pain free" trigger has led us to a deeper emotional understanding of what really matters to that person. When we understand that, we are able to find a more compelling message than "we help relieve pain".

"The real value of your brand connection is created at the deeper level..."

Emotional triggers always relate to this big picture stuff. So ask yourself. How does the problem that you're solving relate and connect to big picture values and issues in your audience's life? We move from 'pain free' to 'big picture' territory surrounding, say, being a great parent or a better person. These intrinsic motivators are powerful because at our core, no matter how rough we appear on the exterior, we are all emotional beings. And we all have powerful, emotional triggers. Neuroscience provides us factual evidence to prove that brands who have an intense emotional attachment win over those who only focus on feature based selling.

Build
Great
Brands

Chapter 4

How brand grows business

Executive Summary

A great brand CAN grow business.

There's no point touching lightly on this topic, which is most likely the reason you picked up this book. Great brands grow great businesses and we explore how in this chapter. We look at brand recognition, brand experience, the sales process, working with sales teams and how to create a value offering that creates conversions from leads.

4.1 The cold hard facts

So now we've begun to form an understanding of what brand is and how we go about developing it, let's spend some time on how brand can grow business explosively. The Design Council UK compared companies who consistently invested into brand versus those over a 10-year period who didn't and found a 200% difference in business growth.

The data, the research and the case studies are clear.
Businesses who invest into brand outperform those who don't.
By inserting strategy before the design process, brands have the opportunity to perform and succeed. But what does success mean? At the beginning of our brand process, I explained that measuring success and setting goals is the only real way you can know how brand has performed for your company. Results must be tangible, measurable, quantitative and consistent. By consistent, I mean that brand is not just a one-off project. It is an ongoing discipline. It must be looked at regularly, much like your accounting. As you grow and evolve, brand must continue to be executed across your business.

"The data, the research and the case studies are clear. Businesses who invest into brand outperform those who don't."

4.2 Why your message matters

We know that brand is a commitment to discover who your audience is, to listen to their needs and to articulate who you are and how you meet those needs.

The very process of discovering this gives you an edge over your competitors because you're getting real insight into how your customers want you to sell to them.

The alternative is to throw marketing and advertising out there like a blindfolded dart player without any formulated strategy or purpose behind you. You just hope that some of it hits but never really know what works and what doesn't.

For example, trialling a direct mailer to an area and then giving up because it didn't work is selling the process short. It may be that the message was not targeted in a way that engaged with the audience. It might have been the wrong area. You then move onto the next tactic convinced that direct mail doesn't work. Only because you didn't look at your core message and brand, the same thing may happen again. Another analogy is with friendships.

The more you know about your friend, and the more time you spend with him, the more likely it is that you'll be able to form a common ground and connection. It's much the same with the relationships you form with your audience.

Some key actions:

1.   Know who your audience is

2.   Understand your audience

3.   Know who you are and how to articulate your offering

4.   Target your message to the needs of your audience

5.   Trial this with your audience and find ways to measure success

4.3 The psychology of a first impression

The dating world gives us some advice here. A good first impression can have a dramatic impact for better or for worse. On a first date we dress our best, wear our best perfume or cologne, shine our shoes, put on our heels and are on our best behaviour because we understand the importance of that first impression.

Have you ever judged a business the moment you've walked through its doors? Of course you have. We are hard wired to do this.
If that first perception is negative, we all know that it is hard work to change it.

A positive first impression for your brand is one of the simplest (and cheapest) things you can focus on. That positive first impression starts you off on the right foot. If your website, or your office space, or your introductory email has already done the hard work to impress, then you can leverage that to build an even more positive experience. This is all part of the sales process and is of course directly related to business growth. Psychological studies reveal that first impressions are formed within seventeen seconds of meeting someone and that 55% of a person's opinion is determined by physical appearance. A further 7% are determined by the words said and 38% from the tone of voice. That's a worthwhile statistic to consider when looking at your company's brand (Silent Messages: Implicit Communication of Emotions and Attitudes, Albert Mehrabian, Wadsworth Publishing, 1972)

Action:

What are the first points of interaction that a potential customer will have with your brand?

- The moment they walk in the door
- Your website
- The way you answer the phone
- The confusing first email you send out to prospects
- The introduction of social media strategy into your engagement
- The introduction pack that you give a prospect

What can you do this week to improve that?

Start by listing the entry points a prospect has into your business and put yourself in their shoes. It might be a little embarrassing when you consider some of these interactions and how uninspiring or negative they might be. You'll find comfort in knowing that everyone who conducts this exercise feels the same, but it becomes liberating when you work out how to improve them.

Spend some time mapping these initial interactions and get the team involved in creative ways they can be improved (this is called customer experience mapping). It could be as simple as thank you cards after first consults, or a more effective website, or more easily explained proposals and point of sale material. It could be a follow up call or packaging redesign that is more colorful. This exercise also allows you to prioritize what will have greatest impact.

4.4 The brand-business performance relationship

Business growth equals two things:

1. Increased revenue
2. Increased value of your business

When we learn to connect brand to business growth (revenue), than we begin to unlock the power that it can have.

You can toil over balance sheets and look over your budget in detail but for business owners and drivers, the most obvious place to achieve business growth is through sales.

The truth is, brand power will command a premium. That's why consumers are willing to spend more money on an Apple iPad compared to less expensive tablets on the market.

HOW DO YOU CONNECT BRAND TO REVENUE?

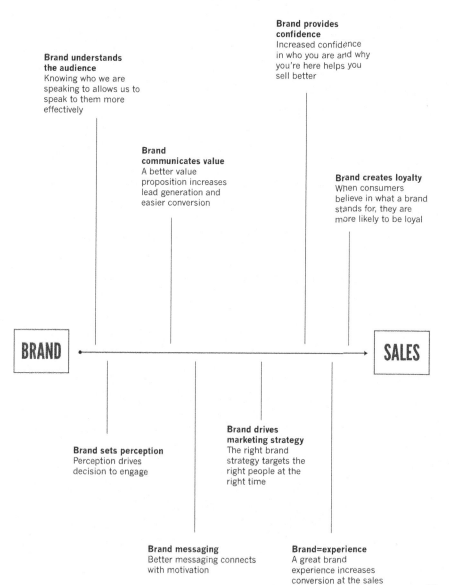

Brand provides confidence
Increased confidence in who you are and why you're here helps you sell better

Brand understands the audience
Knowing who we are speaking to allows us to speak to them more effectively

Brand communicates value
A better value proposition increases lead generation and easier conversion

Brand creates loyalty
When consumers believe in what a brand stands for, they are more likely to be loyal

BRAND → **SALES**

Brand sets perception
Perception drives decision to engage

Brand drives marketing strategy
The right brand strategy targets the right people at the right time

Brand messaging
Better messaging connects with motivation

Brand=experience
A great brand experience increases conversion at the sales

57

Sales is a great way of measuring business performance provided there is capacity to handle the increase in demand and your business model is profitable. There is almost always a bottom line figure that can be used to measure growth and our brand activity must track back to the primary business objectives that are quantified in this way. Again, that's why our first question, when looking at brand, marketing and advertising, is, "How will we define success?". Without knowing the answer to this question, the people involved in the project have no way of understanding what the finish line is.

While brand has many intangible benefits, there must be quantifiable and measurable ones as well. A financial metric helps define the measure of brand success and while not always apparent, there are always ways of finding that number. Brand gives us the ability to look deeply into how we appear to our audience, how we communicate and how we can measure the bottom line impact brand can have on lead generation, conversion of leads, sales and profit.

By increasing our ability to develop a value offering, a set of key messages and a creative direction that is compelling to our audience, the logical outcomes will be an increase in conversions and sales.

A study in the UK by M&C Saatchi found that those brands that were considered desirable outperformed all others in sales growth.

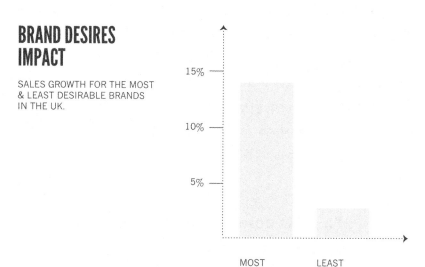

BRAND DESIRES IMPACT

SALES GROWTH FOR THE MOST & LEAST DESIRABLE BRANDS IN THE UK.

4.5 Sales and brand are intimately linked

One of the biggest misconceptions about brand is that it's essentially a creative, fun, touchy-feely kind of exercise. Don't get me wrong, it is these things as well (I can never deny how much I love those mood boards and low-lit lunches where we talk about how we feel), but at its core brand is all about communicating value and trust.

Value is the best gift you can give your sales team. "Price is what you pay, value is what you get" – Warren Buffet.

I believe that the biggest gift we can give a sales process and a sales team is something valuable to sell. There is nothing harder than selling something to someone who doesn't want it. It is important to note here that 'want' and 'desire' are purely perception based. Nobody will 'want' something unless they 'perceive' it to be valuable. We may fall into the trap of blaming our sales team for their performance issues when what we should really be doing is ensuring we give them something valuable to sell. And we understand what is valuable to sell by understanding what the audience perceives as valuable.

"...at its core, brand is all about communicating value and trust."

Do you see Mercedes trying to convince a potential buyer that they are a better financial choice than Toyota? A potential buyer knows the Mercedes is going to cost him or her more than a Toyota, but price is not driving their decision making process. They have already perceived the value in the brand and are consequently willing to pay the price. You're not selling on price anymore. You may have the best product in the world, or an incredibly effective service, but if you can't communicate value to the audience then you don't have anything.

Remember, you are what your customers think you are, not what you think you are. Brand provides value to the sales team in the following areas:

1. A strong, consistent brand that builds trust, rapport and professionalism
2. Messaging and value points that speak directly to the needs, wants and frustrations of the audience
3. Collateral in the form of printed and digital devices that back up what the sales person says and do the job when they're not around

4.6 Perception drives decision

We've all seen a market with products or services that are almost identical and yet there is one that always outsells the others. Why?
The reason is, quite simply, brand.
Remember that one of the purposes of brand is to create differentiation.

Your audience only knows about your produce or service through what others have told them. This is why brand is powerful. It finds a way to articulate a series of messages, communication frameworks and creative directions that compel an audience to choose you over your competitor. Your prospect may be looking at ten websites. They have decided to call only three of them. How do they make their choice? Assume they have no other way to differentiate except through your brand as it is represented on your website. (In reality, of course, there is sometimes word of mouth, other media, possible negative experience with other brands, etc.) Your brand is the only tool they have to make that decision. How many lost customers do you think are out there because your brand did not convince them to contact you over a competitor?

4.7 A sale is a decision

We're learning that brand impacts the sales process. Let's look closer into what a sale is.

A sale is the decision of a prospect to engage with you in exchange for money. At its core, it's a decision.

I've developed this diagram to explain how this decision works from a brand perspective. It helps us explore the psychology of decisions and how brand can have a positive impact on that decision making process.

HOW DOES BRAND IMPACT BUSINESS?

THE BRAND

All the communication devices

CONNECTS WITH

The Brand
The brand is all the communication devices that make up who you are, what you're doing and why you're doing it. This is the way we answer the phone, our brochures, our voice mails, our website – It's everything that communicates us to them.

THE CUSTOMER EXPERIENCE

Their interaction with us

WHICH INFORMS

Customer Experience
This brand connects with our audience. This audience has an experience (a customer experience) based on the type of interactions they have with your brand.

THE BRAND PERCEPTION

What they think of us

WHICH AFFECTS

Brand Perception
This first experience is powerful because it plays a big part in the perception they'll form on who you are – the ongoing experiences help them firm their perceptions on who you are as a company and what they think of you.

CUSTOMER BEHAVIOUR

Their purchasing decision

WHICH DRIVES

Customer Behaviour
This perception is always the driving force behind their behaviour, and specifically their purchasing behaviour. With a negative perception of you, it's unlikely and uncommon that they will purchase what you're selling.

BUSINESS PERFORMANCE

Sales

Business Performance
This decision to purchase is the direct metric on your business sales and revenue, and therein we've simply defined how brand can have a serious and powerful impact on your bottom line growth that you have as a brand.

4.8 Compelling is key

The holy grail of sales is to have a prospect (metaphorically of course) begging you to be a customer. Your product is selling off the shelf. Your phone is ringing off the hook. You don't have enough appointment slots to meet the sales requests. This dream scenario is attainable. The best brands perform well in any economy and in any economic scenario. The best sales processes perform better in times of economic recession. To understand this, I like to use the following table to explain the potential brand scenarios you may find your business in and how it impacts your performance from a sales perspective.

Worst Case	Neutral	Best Case
No Brand You don't have a brand strategy and it shows. It's more difficult to communicate with prospects and convince them to buy because they don't have an impression of your product / service and why it's unique / better.	**No clear consistent view** The market may not have a consistent or informed view and impression of your company, but in your eyes you believe people generally think positively of you.	**It all fits together** Prospects and customers know exactly who you are and what you deliver. It's easy to begin a dialogue with new prospects because they quickly understand what you stand for and are drawn to it.
Contradictions What you do, what you say and how you say it may all contradict each other and send confusing messages to your audience.	**One day** You haven't really thought a lot about branding because it may not seem relevant. You say things like "We could do better but we'll get to that one day". It's clear there is no consistently targeted messaging going out to market.	**Quick close** Deals close quicker because the prospect experience with you continues to consistently support your claims and you are very good and speaking directly to them.
Competitors win Your competitors who communicate more strongly have a better chance of successfully engaging, connecting and taking your prospective customers.	**Neutral** You're not helping yourself but you're also potentially not hurting yourself either.	**Premium prices** You can charge a premium because your market understands and knows why you're better and they're willing to pay for it.

For me, the depth at which brand impacts business performance and bottom line profit means that no matter what the business, a decision to not invest in brand is always a missed opportunity for business growth.

Summary points

1. Understanding your audience enables you to target your branding more effectively towards their needs
2. When your message connects with your audience and their needs, the sales process is easier because there is perceived value
3. Better brands help sales teams because branding collateral is an imperative part of a sales person's toolkit. What they say can only go so far. The collateral enables them to back it up with professionalism and creative engagement

**Build
Great
Brands**

Chapter 5

You've got a brand problem when...

Executive Summary

We've all got a "friend" who has a brand problem...

The signs of an under-performing brand are clear. Once we identify that we can do better then we have an opportunity to unlock the potential that's been waiting for our business. This chapter uncovers the top ten signs that you have a brand problem and how brand can help in each of them

5.1 What's a brand problem?

So by now, we know what a brand is.

We understand its value to our business (fingers crossed).

We believe in its ability to impact business performance.

But how do we evaluate whether we are in need of a brand overhaul or a re-brand?

Well, if you agree with me in believing that great brands make the world a better place, then by default, it must be assumed and believed that bad brands make the world a worse off place:

- Bad brands are non-imaginative.
- They fail to differentiate
- They don't inspire internally (the company)
- They don't inspire externally (the clients)
- They fail to engage with their audience
- They undermine the sales effort
- They are embarrassing – and embarrassing is not what you want to feel about your own company!

There are some textbook scenarios that I like to define as: "That moment when you know you have a brand problem". It might not always be recognisable straight away but pretty soon it becomes painfully clear over a period of time (or even in an instant) that a brand problem exists and that it must be faced, if the company is to move forward.

A brand problem is nothing to be ashamed of. In fact I think in some ways we all have one. Even the biggest companies in the world continue to work on their brand, because they understand the importance of brand maintenance to their success.

The benefits of acting on a brand problem go beyond business growth and you may be surprised to hear why. People come to work with a new sense of pride for the organization and the atmosphere begins to change. Customers engage better with the organization and loyalty is fostered. Potential all-star employees begin contacting you to see if you have positions available. The follow on benefits can be even more transforming than the fiscal goal.

"A brand problem is nothing to be ashamed of."

5.2 The Ten Signs

In your quest to build a great business you know you've got a brand problem when some of the symptoms of bad brands begin to surface. They take the form of common scenarios that are worth looking out for in your own business and the businesses of your friends, because a word of advice around improving your friend's brand may just be the lifeline they need.

Importantly, it's not always the struggling companies that have a brand problem. What I love seeing is a company with great performance but bad branding. What it highlights to me is the potential opportunity for even more growth that they are missing out on. Imagine if their brand were on message, directed to their audience and articulated perfectly both in value proposition and creative. They have successfully grown and continue to grow despite their brand – imagine if they invested into doing branding right. This is an important factor to take into consideration. Brand isn't your last ditch attempt to keep your company afloat. It's an investment and one that is applicable and relevant at any stage of a business growth cycle.

Here are the ten 'brand symptoms' that help guide the question
'Do I have a brand problem?'

1. The misconception:

A misconception amongst your audience and/or team about what kind of company you are and what you really do. When you ask your team or clients to describe your business, the answers are very different. Clients and/or team members often say; " Really?? I didn't know you/we did that". You overhear someone on your team speaking to a prospect on the phone and the way they talk about the company is not in line with how you feel it should be represented.

2. Negative referrals:

Poorly managed customer and community interaction by previous management leading to negative referrals and a little bit of bad talk going on around town. You find yourself having to explain the past by saying "No don't worry, we're not like that anymore" You're too scared to call old clients.

3. A start-up without a plan:

You're a start-up with a great idea but no idea how to connect with the market – you're stuck. You often sit at your desk with a blank piece of paper thinking to yourself "Ok...what next?" You get the funny feeling you're too busy doing stuff but not important stuff.

If asked, you wouldn't feel comfortable describing your business in 10 seconds to a stranger.

4. New product. New market:

Your business is pivoting its product/service offering or entering a new market space and needs to reposition its brand to align with your new audience or more clearly communicate your new offering. You've changed product/service or pricing/value offering and the new market is quite different to the old one.

5. Quick growth. Old brand:

Your company has grown through market opportunity but the brand has not caught up with it. You're still using the logo your brother's uncle's dog did for you in Microsoft Paint and it's becoming a little bit of a roadblock to moving forward. Your website still has © 2002 on the footer.

6. Ashamed of your brand family:

You feel embarrassed about your current logo, business card and website. You get that sinking feeling in your stomach when someone asks for your business card, or wants to visit your website. (This for me has to be one of the worst feelings ever).

7. Where did the logo go?

You have stopped using your branding for fear that it's losing you work. You find yourself deleting your website off your email footer for fear that someone may actually visit the site and read the completely out of date content.

8. Diversification:

You are diversifying your business and in need of a new brand or sub brand. You've started a new product line / business within your business without any kind of brand positioning and you're not too sure how to get the word out there whilst keeping separation from your core business.

9. So many competitors:

You exist within a congested and flooded market with competitors all offering a similar service. You feel that you're different but your brand doesn't communicate any kind of differentiation from those competitors. When you look at your brand next to your competitors, it doesn't seem to stand out. Secondly, you have no real messaging of any value around why you're different to your competitor and it makes it hard to win pitches on anything but price. 100% commitment to customer service is the only point of differentiation you can think of when you brainstorm.

10. Time to raise prices:

Your prices have had to stay down because you cannot succeed when they are higher. This is because your brand is not building loyalty and communicating you as a premium provider; and for this reason, it cannot demand a price premium. You dream of putting your prices up but can't seem to find a way to communicate the increased value your customers will receive.

"Brand isn't your last ditch attempt to keep your company afloat."

5.3 Where brand can help

In all these scenarios and more, brand creates an environment and forum to explore the reasoning behind why these problems exist and create a pathway to a solution. Outside assistance is often helpful in these times. Consider this checklist below to help in your process when considering whether brand can have an impact for you.

The right people are the ones that have the right process

The right brand process forces you to ask questions you haven't asked before and in those questions you get answers relating to how best to engage with an audience that needs whatever it is that you do.

Everyone is selling something deeper than what they think

Everyone is selling something, no matter what you do: Brand gives us the opportunity to articulate our selling proposition in a way that engages with the needs, frustrations and wants of our audience and to do it consistently. Our selling point isn't "what we do" but "what emotional value" we provide when the transaction takes place. This is always more powerful.

Consistency

Great brands demand consistency and consistency helps build perception just as repetition breeds habit. Social psychology is the foundation for the identity-based brand management model. If we hear and see something regularly, we become more inclined to believe and align with it.

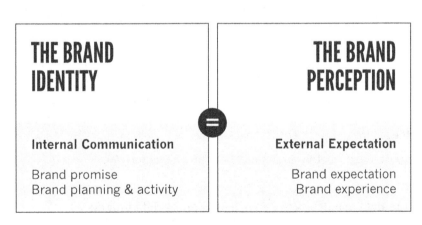

Consistent and continuous behaviour alongside communication leads to strong perceptions. Hearing it once is often not enough. Hearing it continually and having it reinforced with a brand experience is key.

Consistency has two major components:

1. Define who you are to your audience in a way that connects with them

2. Consistently deliver that message creatively and with discipline

If done well, this will lead to a unified belief in your business. When customers experience an inauthentic or inconsistent message from a brand, it builds distrust, and eventually dislike, followed by disloyalty. Conversely, when they have positive interactions, it builds trust and loyalty. Consistency of message, service, brand and authenticity are the key to winning your market.

Objectivity: A fresh perspective

An outside creative and strategic opinion gives you a view on your business that you haven't had before and that refreshing approach leads to a message and story that can leverage creatively.

Profit Profit Profit

Bottom line profits result from purchasing decisions, and purchasing decisions are impacted by brand.

Value Value Value

Brand currency increases the value of a company by having a documented, measured and successful brand approach. A business that leverages its brand is intrinsically more powerful to prospective buyers of your business.

Include your stakeholders

If you work within an organization, then this book and specifically this chapter is a really useful resource for your decision-makers to read.

If you are a business owner who has not yet tapped into the power and potential of branding, then it may be time to consider that you may have a brand opportunity and to start investing into one of the most rewarding processes that your company can undergo.

5.0 You've got a brand problem when...

Build
Great
Brands

Chapter 6

Branding is changing in the 21st century

Executive Summary

The times are a-changing
There are four primary reasons that brand will continue to change in
the 21st century and they've all go to do with people. There is more
choice. There are more problems. Consumers want relationships and
connection. And, finally, there is globalization.

6.1 Reason one: More choice

It used to be different. "Buy our 99c soup" was all you needed as your slogan to sell. Competition was low and decision-making for products seemed grounded in surface level (tier one) needs.

With fewer options to choose from, you could get away with just being present on the supermarket shelf. Today, things are different. Consumers struggle to make decisions because of what we refer to as option overload. Option overload is a common problem for consumers (and hence brands) because the logical decision-making processes that we've relied on for years no longer work. The market is now flooded with choice and consumers can't possibly try everything to know which one is best. They can't taste all the soups and there is now such a variety of price (often within just a matter of cents of each other) that it makes it difficult to understand which choice is best.

So what do you do when you don't know what to choose? You use the mechanism of brand to help you make the choice. When we apply that to something as simple as ice cream, we can see the results. The every day consumer has little or no idea what differentiates one product from another until they try it. But the allure of a new brand can be quite compelling. Aside from blindfolding yourself, spinning around five times and randomly pointing, a decision-making framework must be formed quickly in order to make a choice. In these situations, you turn to something like brand to discover differentiation. Brand becomes your friend; no, your savior!

Something as simple as packaging can be the difference between purchasing good or bad ice cream (in your own mind) – it can drive your decision to impress friends whose dinner party you're attending or play to your values of "simple works best". The product itself is irrelevant because there's no way of judging it (for the initial purchase). It is the branding that helps you make that first trial.

History is full of examples with companies experiencing diminishing sales from tired brands, Brands who successfully refresh their image and packaging have experienced staggering results. When artisan ice cream brand Van Leeuwen re-branded their packaging, customer's starting taking photos and sharing them on social media. The product

was already exceptional but it wasn't until the packaging redesign that sales soared 50%. In fact, the company received endless feedback from customers purchasing based purely on the multi colored design.

6.2 Reason two: More problems

The second reason brand is changing in the 21st Century is that it now has to solve more problems than ever.

Brands must communicate how we as businesses solve the problems of our market. Ask yourself "What problem am I solving?" And then "Would I pay money to solve that problem?"

"Ask yourself 'What problem am I solving?'..."

It's a confronting question and if the answer to question two is, "no", then you haven't found the right way to articulate the real problem that you sell a solution for.

A hundred years ago we led simpler lives and our problems were simply defined. Fewer solutions existed as fewer solutions were needed. The general store was all you needed and your accountant, your lawyer and your banker were your only consultants. Now needs have widened and the number of defined problems has expanded. When brands don't correctly define what they do and who they are as problem solvers to their audience, the potential customer is left scratching his or her head. They don't really know what you're doing for them. The reason for this is that there has been no attempt to educate that person on whether you solve a problem that they identify with. All they know is that they don't really understand what you do, why you do it and why they should care. With their problem unsolved, they turn to somewhere else. If branded better, that problem may have been solved in a second and sales could have followed.

With an increase in competitors, complexity of problems and an overwhelming amount of advertising, effective branding is essential to cut through noise and to tell your customer why you matter. When they can understand and value what you're selling, research suggests that the price matters little.

"Your premium brand had better be delivering something special or it's not going to get the business." – Warren Buffet.

6.3 Reason three: Relationship vs. Transaction

In today's society, with community becoming more and more digitized, there is a growing concern and hunger for consumers to know and understand the brands they engage with. They want a connection and a relationship – not just a sales pitch.

Social and global responsibility is now an important part of branding. This is because of what I call the 'generational handover'. As Gen X, Gen Y and Millennials take the stage as income earners and mid to upper level management, their values will cascade down into all consumer behaviour. They will breed a workforce and generation of similarly minded people who care about more than just what you do, but how you do it, why you do it and how you're making the world a better place while doing it. This is driven from a hunger to form connections, not transactions. They choose where they invest their money and are conscious about their actions contributing either negatively or positively to their planet and their economy. Being a part of the change, not the problem, is central to all Gen X / Gen Y world views.

So what does it mean to have a relationship and how do you form a connection whether you're an accountant, a food chain, a supermarket or a consultant? Relationship based branding occurs on many different levels depending on what industry you're in (I.e. Does a client really want to be Facebook friends with their lawyer?) but as a whole, the ability to connect on something deeper than service and product quality

"When you align your values with those of your audience, loyalty develops."

provides a more powerful legacy of loyalty for those brands that decide to engage in this way.

Brand connection and relationship is driven by trust, consistency, accessibility, active listening, responding to needs, authenticity, integrity and sharing common values. When you align your values with those of your audience, loyalty develops. They care about what you care about.

Jeff Bezos, of Kindle and Amazon fame, says, "Your brand is formed primarily, not by what your company says about itself, but what the company does."

Your consumers want to know 'the why' behind 'the what' and this is now a major angle in all brand consulting. It's in your singular story that no one else can replicate that you find a unique edge against competition. Your why is driven by your story and your story is undeniably "you". That unique story cannot be replicated.

Connection and relationship is the powerful way that brand can push past too much choice and provide hooks for consumers to connect with.

When you master this ability to connect as a brand, you achieve what only the very best brands achieve: the ability to empower a consumer to feel better about themselves after engaging with you. Think about that for a second and imagine what kind of loyalty you can build when a consumer feels like that.

6.4 Reason 4: Globalization

Globalization is essentially the world feeling smaller. It is the overall movement towards connected economics, marketplaces and social activities. There's no place to hide as a brand these days. Your brand and the information surrounding it is accessible 24 hours a day, 365 days a year. More than ever, it is difficult to control the forums and contexts in which you will be seen. Globalization has turned branding into a 360-degree activity rather than a one-dimensional schedule of marketing plans, billboards and TV. For this reason, there needs to be consistent interaction with your customers.

The New York Times reported that we are inundated with as many as 20,000 individual messages every day from advertising. They may not be directly competing with you as a brand but they are certainly creating 'noise'. From an advertising perspective, in an average day, Scott M Davis reports that we are exposed to six thousand advertisements and to more than twenty five thousand new products.

What does globalization mean for branding? It means we have the potential to engage with our audience more regularly and to achieve a wider reach than ever before. But without an effective brand, we are just adding to the noise. With the opportunity for acceptable and economical consistent communication, there is less need for shouting and more pleasure in talking. It's time to use the mediums and channels available to you to have a conversation with your customers and not (just) to shout at them.

6.0 Branding is changing in the 21st Century

Build
Great
Brands

Chapter 7

Brand authenticity

Executive Summary

More human please

Some practical help and tips on why and how to insert authenticity into branding. This chapter challenges you to find the purpose, heart and (higher) calling of your brand, and why your customers should want to know about this.

What is brand authenticity? It refers to the ability of a brand to communicate who and what it is to the market. It is engaging, sincere and trustworthy. As we have seen, people are attracted to authenticity, especially in a market flooded by choice. This choice drives us to connect with the safe, the certain, the trustworthy and the real. It comes as a result of a consumer group looking for more meaningful transactions.

7.1 No more corporate speak

As we progress further into the 2000's, big brands are overhauling the way they speak and developing human-to-human focused protocols. It's all about speaking to people on their level. Gen X, Gen Y and the Millennials all value collaboration and want things easy, simple and designed around decisive action. This has had a direct impact on branding, advertising and the way that brands speak to their audiences.

This new generation of consumers is sick of corporate speak. They crave human connection. They crave community. They long to get deals done by talking through things honestly and authentically. This new generation of business owners, managers, workers and consumers are begging brands to talk more like humans, please. The corporate robot is cold, too sales-focused and they see right through it. Everyday language is the new business pitch. Too professional is professional no more.

We need to connect with our customers in everyday language that talks across and not down to the reader. People are educated, savvier, willing and wanting to be treated as equals. It is because of this that brands must deconstruct the complex talk that has clouded their manuals, their brochures, their websites and their sales pitches.

In this fast-paced, multi-dimensional and overcrowded society, it is important to create efficient and engaging messaging for consumers. Throw in some fun, some authenticity and a little bit of personality, and boy oh boy – you've got yourself a brand.

Your action. It's time to group and collate everything that you use to communicate with your audience. Websites, brochures, email templates, proposals. Then go through the 'humanize' activity in one of the following chapters (8.7).

"Big brands are overhauling the way they speak and developing human-to-human focused protocols."

7.2 Date your customer

Sooner or later you have to reveal your cards to your customer. But this is a good thing because it forces honesty. You can go on a couple of blind dates but it's not until you actually open up and show someone who you are and what you stand for that they can fall in love with you.

And so it is with branding. Letting your customer get to know you and showing an active interest in who they are results in them forming a stronger connection with you as an organization.

7.3 Integrity, ethics and all that stuff

Authenticity is now the name of the game. People like the fact that you're not afraid to show a little transparency and that you're trying to make the world a better place. They're not expecting the corporate, clean, professional approach.

Is this in the sales manuals you buy? Maybe not but they were probably written twenty years ago anyway. Look at any advertising and brand activity from the most recognized brands in the world. Their focus is on community, human connection and honesty, not on "we're the biggest and the best". These brands have recognized that being corporate repulses many of their consumers who want to be treated as an individual not a number.

This authenticity is paving the way for branding to make the world a better place by forcing the companies we work with to ensure that at the core of everything they do, there is an authentic voice of integrity, reliability, honesty and ethics. Just as in the scenario of dating, you can only be you.

"Authenticity is the name of the game"

7.4 Get a core purpose

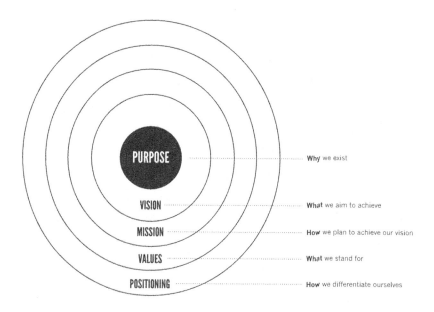

The most pertinent question your organization can ask is, "Why do we exist?" Your core purpose is a brand-able part of your organization. This is not a mission or vision statement or even a set of company values. It is the center from which your whole company can act; the big 'why' behind your 'what'. It is bigger and deeper than any goal you can set. Core purpose is where stakeholders find their deepest emotional connection with your brand. It attracts alliances, loyal customers and talented candidates for careers.

For Disney, their core purpose is, "make people happy". It isn't fancy but it aligns with every single person that works for this $42 billion company. It is the overarching purpose behind all their roles. To make people happy.

3M's core purpose is, "solving ordinary problems innovatively."
Nike's is, "experience the emotion of winning while crushing your competition." You'll notice that the branding, messaging and advertising surrounding these brands aligns perfectly with these core purpose statements. Further than that, they have nailed their audience. They know exactly who they are · and who they aren't.

A core purpose has the ability to last forever. Ours at the branding company I started is, "Build great brands". It is central to what we're doing now and what we'll be doing in the future and it's our statement of how we intend to make the world a better place.
Here's a method to help you develop or re-define yours:

- Start by developing a statement that describes your company.
- Ask yourself, "Why are we important to our customers, and to our market?"
- Ask yourself, "Why is this important?" Keep asking this question.
- Make your statement as simple as you can. You're trying to filter your statement down to one thing.

Filter down this message till you get to purest form of "Why" you can think of.

7.5 Developing brand value statements

Your research into your audience, your values, how you intend to change the world and your core purpose should end with the culmination of a series of brand value statements that will determine your tone and message. You will never use them in a brochure or a website promotional piece but they will become great drivers for your brand creation process and a reference point at each stage of your branding and advertising.

"The most pertinent question your organization can ask is, 'Why do we exist?"

Here are some further principles:

1. Brand statements often start with "We..." because they collectively describe your organization
2. You'll never use them in public so don't worry about how they sound.
3. Their primary function is to define what your brand must communicate.
4. The truer they are, the easier it'll be to use them as filters when moving through a branding process
5. They must mean something to you.

7.6 Find a way to change the world

Trust me on this. Find a way to change the world. Don't fight it. Any little way – it doesn't matter. By changing the world, you will make your brand about something bigger than you. When you give consumers the opportunity to take part in something bigger than themselves, they join a movement and a cause, and this becomes something that transcends the basic "I pay money for your product or your service" relationship. It can be powerfully simple.

The way we change the world relates intrinsically to our core purpose and links powerfully to our story. It is not separate from these things but rather, these things reaffirm this core purpose in the minds of our audience.

Once you have this defined, use it within your branding. Give your audience something to connect with. By engaging with you as a company, they are contributing to your purpose in changing the world to make it a better place. This is an authentically attractive selling point for your audience.

"Trust me on this. Find a way to change the world. Don't fight it."

7.7 Turn your transaction into an experience

Apple took this to another level when designing their new retail stores, complete with free genius bars, nifty mobile payment devices and lots and lots of staff wearing those blue t-shirts. Apple is totally customer-focused from the moment you step foot inside their door. Their results are undeniable. Apple retail stores have become a phenomenon across the planet, helping generate fierce customer loyalty and delivering on Apple's promise to change the world through beautifully designed products and experiences.

Consistency is key and one of the best ways to deliver a consistent brand across the entire customer experience is to map the points of connection that make up your entire interaction with a prospect or customer (there I go mentioning customer experience mapping again).

It starts all the way back when they first hear about you. This is way before the moment they hand over their credit card. (In fact, the payment is the least important point of the experience.)

When we create a customer experience map, we aim to understand each potential point of interaction that a consumer will have with our organization and brainstorm ways to improve that brand experience. The authentic moments that 'wow' the customer and build a more positive perception of the brand.

**Build
Great
Brands**

Chapter 8

The toolkit

Executive Summary

Exercises to get you started now.

Practical exercises to get you and your team started on building an even greater brand.

8.1 Time to get practical

These exercises will get you thinking about your brand, your audience and how to bridge the gap between. Go through them over a coffee, while listening to Jazz and, hopefully, looking out over an ocean or a lake. Don't do it in your office when you've got ten minutes spare before your next meeting. Brand is a scientific and creative process so you need time, space, room and freedom to combine the two.

Also, run through some of these exercises with your team. When you do engage with a brand agency down the track, these exercises will give you an incredible amount of insight when they start to ask similar questions.

Share these exercises with your colleagues and friends: there are downloadable copies at www.buildgreatbrands.com

8.2 Conduct your own brand audit exercise

This exercise provides an initial survey of where things are at the moment and it's a great place to start.

Collate the following information surrounding your brand, your marketplace and your audience. Create a list of all these items with a score out of 10 on the effectiveness of each.

Information about us

- What industry are we in?
- Who are our three major competitors (direct)?
- Do we have any indirect competitors?
- Compare their logos to ours (print them out and discuss)
- Compare their websites to ours (print them out and discuss)
- What groups can we split our customers into?
- Where are we placed if we had to compare the market based only on price?
- Where are we placed if we had to compare the market based only on quality of product / service?

Messaging

- Do we have any slogans?
- Do we have any fall back selling lines that we use?
- What are our three major selling features?
- Do we have a brand promise?

Our collateral

The pieces that visually communicate our brand: collate and print out to display

- Logo
- Key color swatches
- Stationery
- Point of sale material
- Brochures
- Flyers
- Event leaflets
- Newspaper and publication ads
- Case studies
- Presentation templates / PowerPoint
- Newsletters
- Proposal covers

- Website print out
- Email signature
- Video content
- Social media pages and channels
- Blogs
- Online display ads
- Pay per click ads

- Loyalty cards
- Direct mail pieces done in the past
- Packaging
- Radio ads

Marketing insights

- How would we describe the marketing approach of our organization?
- What are our marketing objectives?
- Are any of our marketing objectives not sales related?
- What is our biggest problem / challenge when it comes to marketing?
- Who controls the marketing? Do we have a plan? Is it followed?

- How do we currently communicate with customers?

    1. Current customers
    2. Lost customers
    3. Loyal customers
    4. Prospective customers

- What of the following marketing activities have you done, and to what success?

    1. Events
    2. Press
    3. Radio
    4. TV
    5. Outdoor
    6. Sponsorship
    7. Public Relations
    8. Social media
    9. Direct Mail
    10. Electronic Direct Mail
    11. SEO
    12. Search engine marketing
    13. Educational seminars
    14. Customer relationship teams
    15. Awards
    16. Case studies
    17. Loyalty programs
    18. Newsletters

8.3 Who and why?

This activity is extremely revealing and undeniably scary.
We want to decide who our best customers are, and why they like us.

1. Who are our three most profitable clients / customers /
    customer groups? (Notice I said profitable, not biggest)

2. Who are our three favorite clients / customers / customer
    groups? Are they different to the ones in the first answer?

3. If B2C (business to consumer), describe that person. If B2B
    (business to business), who is the specific person(s) we deal
    with within our ideal business?

4. What about them makes them our favorite?

5. What % of our clientele match a similar profile?

6. Can we interview them and ask them:

*   Why did you begin using us?
*   Why do you continue to use us?
*   What is our best selling point?
*   Do you tell others about us? If so, who? If not, why not?
*   Does anything about how we do things frustrate them?
*   What should we stop doing / keep doing and start doing?

8.4 Finding a core purpose

Building Your Company's Vision by Jim Collins and Jerry Porras (Harvard Review) is one of the best guides about centering your organization on a purpose.

8.5 How to fill out the brand pyramid:
Creating a purpose and plan for your brand

The brand pyramid offers a bird's eye view of our brand purpose. What are we trying to achieve as a brand and how do we trace this back to annually, quarterly and daily activities in our quest to achieve that. This is a great way of determining daily priorities based on big picture directions.

You can download this as a PDF at www.buildgreatbrands.com.

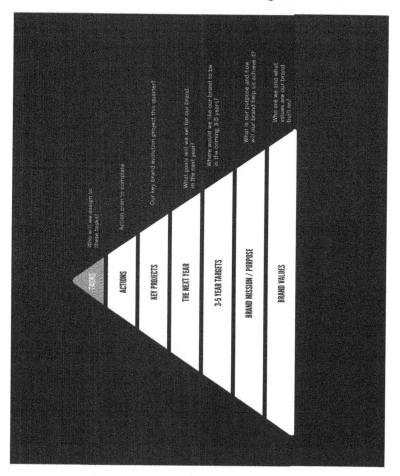

8.6 Ten questions to brainstorm with your team

Record these results (anonymously if you want to) and there will be some invaluable information you will discover from this activity. Remember, your brand is as important to your team as it is for your customers. What they think matters.

1. What do we do?

Write down on a piece of paper what we do as a company in one sentence:

- Now show it to everyone
- Are they different? How different?
- Has anyone articulated it really well?
- What key words can we take from each person's version?

ACTION

Re-work a version that resonates with the company (you can bring in outside help if words aren't your thing), then share it with your team. You'll have an idea of whether it works or not by their reaction.

2. Our current audience

Who do we think our audience is?

3. Our ideal clients

Write out who our top ten ideal clients are currently.

4. Our ideal audience

Who is our ideal audience (who do you want to deal with) and who isn't?

Write out the top potential client / customer groups we'd like to deal with.

5. The difference

Is there a difference between our current and ideal? What is that difference and why?

6. The one thing

If you had to make this company better today with one thing, what would you do?

7. Our current brand

What do you think of our brand? How does it make you feel?

8. What do others think?

What do your friends and family say when you show it to them? What??!! You don't show it to them? Ok, what would they say?

9. How do we compare?

*   How does our brand compare (not our product/service/offering) to competitors?
*   Who is doing this better than us?
*   Ask the team – they'll be honest.
*   Let's go look at our competitors (top 5) and compare websites / brand / message together

10. If we were a brand...

If we were a brand of car within the market, what would we be and why? This is an age-old advertising question and I don't care for the answer so much as the reasons for the answer. It's a great way to gauge how you and your team see yourselves.

8.7 Humanize!

People want brands and brand experiences to be humanized, enjoyable, authentic and real. When we pursue this within our own organizations, we create a brand experience worth writing home about.

Messaging

Gather all the text on your website and in your brochures, on your emails etc...

Go through each part, listening to the 'flavor' of the words and brainstorm how to humanize it. How can we authentically speak the language of 'human' to people instead of stale corporate vernacular?

Human contact

Some questions to ask yourself and your team to encourage more discussion:

1. Are you still using an info@ email address?
2. Have you read your legal terms lately?
3. Are your terms in small font?
4. Have you listened to the way your team answers the phone?
5. Do you have a language document to help everyone understand how best to speak to customers? Apple does.
6. Are the emails you send out corporate and stale, or can they have personality?
7. What do your vacation/holiday responders sound like?
8. Do you just talk to your customers to find out how to get better?
9. Are the rules the rules, or do people have autonomy to bend them a little bit to keep customers happy?
10. Is your sales process based on customer problem solving or company profit generation?

Experience

What are three things we can do to fulfil each of the following humanising goals for our brand experience

1. Helping our customers feel listened to and understood
2. Sounding like a person and not a robot
3. Transparency to all
4. Being interesting and not boring
5. Empowering our team to be both 100% authentic and 100% brand ambassadors
6. Providing pleasant surprises for our customers when they least expect it

8.8 Customer experience mapping

A brand experience is made up of many different and immersive interactions.

Fill in the diagram

We fill out the diagram below by listing the many different interactions (in order) that will occur throughout the life of a customer's brand experience. It is important that we don't under value any interaction that we perceive to be of little significance. They are all important and to be considered.

Brainstorm interaction improvement

Each interaction has the potential to be improved. Your task is to brainstorm how you can do that. It might be something little or something large and it might not relate to increased product delivery or service. What it does is add 'wow' factor to the experience.

When brainstorming, consider these following aspects of a brand experience:

1.	Look	How our brand looks
2.	Feel	How our brand engages the senses (sound, scent)
3.	Talk	What is the voice of our brand? How do we sound, what is our style of language?
4.	Act	How do we act with customers and each other and how does this represent our brand?
5.	Atmosphere	Our workplace and our places of interaction. How are they branded to align with our values?
6.	Digital	How we interact via the digital senses as it pertains to fun and functionality. Evaluate the interactivity and intuitiveness.
7.	Conversational	The dialogue: How we listen and respond to the needs and requests of our audience. Are we still human?

BRAND AWARENESS

They hear about us or see us for the first time

1.
2.
3.
4.
5.

BRAND INTRODUCTION

The first contact they make

1.
2.
3.
4.
5.

BRAND EXPERIENCE

The sales process to win them over

1.
2.
3.
4.
5.

BRAND CONVERSION

The conversion and the delivery

1.
2.
3.
4.
5.

BRAND LOYALTY

Enticing them to continue to use us

1.
2.
3.
4.
5.

BRAND ADVOCACY

They spread the word

1.
2.
3.
4.
5.

8.9 Connecting your values to your logo

A brand starts with an understanding of who your organization is and finishes as a brand experience made up of many different elements. However, the initial element that anchors a brand is the logo, which must embody the values and truths of your brand. To ensure that you start off on the right foot, use this worksheet to:

- Discover whether your logo embodies your values and directions
- Start the process of developing a visual brand

Start from the bottom and work your way up. Use post-it notes if you wish.

1. Understanding who we are:
Compresses all your research, soul searching and purpose defining from the first stage into some defining keywords and sentences about who you are as a brand. At this point, they remain broad in nature.

2. Defining core messages:
These relate to your brand values. They are not customer facing but internal facing and define for you what the brand needs to communicate and say. It is the heart of who you are as a brand. Come up with four or five easy to understand statements.

3. Targeted messages:
The core messages are not enough. There must be an evolution towards messages targeted and directed specifically to your audience. Their needs, wants and frustrations must be considered, as engagement is the key.

4. Look and feel:
At this point, we move towards the creative side of our brain in visualising what these steps beforehand mean for our brand as it relates to tone and feel. Will our look and feel be light or dark? Will it be bold or soft? What kind of imagery will it have? What will its tone of voice be?

5. The logo:
Now that we have a broad understanding of what the brand will look and feel like, what does this mean for the logo? Get specific here and consider fonts, colors, angles, shapes, sharp edges, soft edges and comparative brands that embody similar values in other industries. The goal is to be directional and specific.

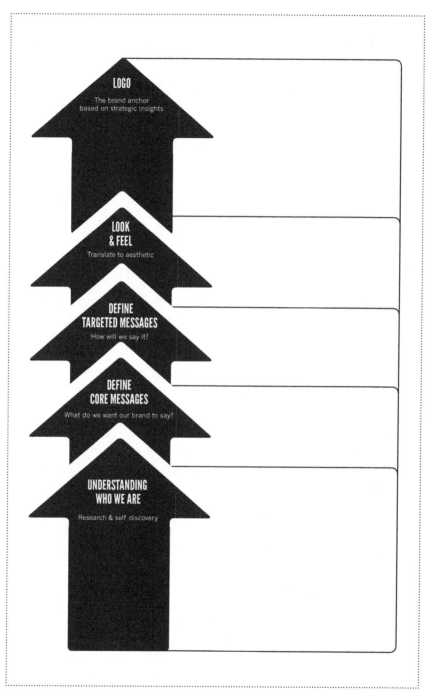

LOGO

The brand anchor
based on strategic insights

**LOOK
& FEEL**

Translate to aesthetic

**DEFINE
TARGETED MESSAGES**

How will we say it?

**DEFINE
CORE MESSAGES**

What do we want our brand to say?

**UNDERSTANDING
WHO WE ARE**

Research & self discovery

8.10 Weekly brand checklist

A weekly checklist is a great place for a marketing manager or CMO to start with ensuring that the brand is remaining on target:

Know the gaps

Are there any gaps between where we want our brand to be and where it is now?
If so, where are these gaps present?
How will we tackle solving these gaps in the next ____ days/months?

Engage the team

How are we engaging our team with understanding, embodying and spreading the brand in the right way?

Numbers

What are our key numbers to measure the success of our brand and marketing?

Feedback

What feedback are we receiving about our brand this week/month?
Go through the brand collateral list to use as a guide
Is it good or bad feedback?
What are our customers saying about us as an organization?

The confidence test

How confident are we in displaying our brand at meetings and events?
How do I feel when someone asks to check out our website?
When was the last time we read through all the content in our brochures and on our website to ensure it aligned with who we are and what we do?

Improve the experience

What one thing can we do this week/month to improve the brand experience for our audience?

8.11 Setting up brand metrics

It's time to create a metrics system to measure your brand and your marketing activities. This is one of the best ways to ensure that brand is connected to business performance.

Don't get stuck in the marketing rut of not knowing where your leads are coming from and not understanding what activity is most effective in achieving your goals.

A metrics system allows you to pinpoint where your best customers come from and what strategies are most effective. It also helps you understand how much a client is worth to you and how much you pay to acquire them.

First step: identify what's working.

Source of leads

- Where do my good customers come from?
- Where do my bad customers come from?
- What activity is costing me money but not generating outcomes?

Conversion and ROI

- How well do we convert from lead to transaction?
- What is the average time it takes to do this?
- Do they come back?

Do I mind?

- What am I willing to spend money on because it has qualitative value (even if not quantitative)?

Awareness

- Who knows about us?

Second step: Drill down into your lead generation

1. List your top ten performing customers in the last twelve months, where they came from and how you acquired them.
2. What is this caliber of customer worth to you?
3. How many transactions would you expect to receive from them and at what frequency?
4. What is the lifetime value of this customer?

#	Customer	Lead source	$ value 1st	Qty transactions	$ Value life
1					
2					
3					
4					
5					
6					
7					
8					
9					
10					

Step three: Map your activity and understand what is converting

1. What activity are we doing to acquire more business? What are we spending on those activities and what results are we currently experiencing?
2. What is our current conversion rate from enquiry to transaction per activity (if measurable)?
3. What are the primary reasons we know that we're not converting?
4. How can we improve on that conversion? Who is doing this better than us?

Marketing Activity	$ Spend per Month	Qty Leads	Qty Conversions	$ Value Conversions

Marketing Activity	Cost per lead ($/Qty)	Conversion %	ROI ($ spend / (Qty Conversions x $ Value Conversions))

Step four: Make a budget

1. What are we willing to spend to acquire one customer?
2. Based on our budget and ROI, are we willing to spend 10, 20, 30% of the year one value of that customer?
3. What is an industry benchmark? Are the figures available?
4. How many new customers would we like in the next twelve months?

New customers x acceptable cost per acquisition value = $ Budget

i.e. 100 new clients worth $10,000 each to use = $1,000,000
We are willing to spend 20% of that value to acquire those customers.

Marketing budget $200,000
Potential earnings from new $1,000,000
Net profit before costs of goods $800,000   =   4:1 ROI

What is a conversion / customer worth to us?	$
How many conversions do we want to achieve?	Qty
What's that worth to us collectively in revenue?	$
What % of value are we willing to spend to acquire?	%
This equates to a total amount per customer of	$

Now that we know (a) how many conversions we want and (b) what we're willing to pay for those conversions each, we have a marketing budget (a x b)

Our marketing budget is...	$

Step five: Trial marketing activities and measure performance

1. List what marketing activities you'll be trialling for the month
2. Define the intended results for each
3. How will creative and messaging contribute to these results?
4. How will we measure the effectiveness of these activities?

   Some ideas may be 1300 number tracking, coupon tracking, a specific call to action, code words to activate discounts, vertical channel targeting

Step six: Monthly brainstorm how to improve on your entire brand management

Use the table below as a guideline for brainstorming strategies, activities and tweaks to your campaigns to improve leads, conversions and repeat spend.

Marketing activity to trial	Leads	Conversions	Repeat spend
Better marketing activity			
Better brand positioning			
Better messaging			
More engaging creative			
Better call to action			
Better value proposition			
Better cross sell / up sell			

8.12 Trade secrets

You'll want to know about these when it comes to branding:

Not all equal
Not all agencies are equal – don't just pick one out of a hat. They won't all do a great job.

What's the process?
Ask to see their process on branding. If they don't have a process, then they're likely not the right agency for you.

You're working with people
Relationship is key: You need to feel comfortable with who you're dealing with – it needs to trump price because ultimately, this is an investment that should bring a return and it's the kind of journey that you want to do with a company that you like and who you believe in.

You need a timeline
Ask for a timeline - if they don't have a project plan and timeline, be worried.

When it goes over time
There are so many reasons for projects to run over time (some may be caused by you) but if an agency promises you the world with an over ambitious timeline, then be prepared for potential disappointment because it could be unrealistic.

Trust the process
It's not going to be the perfect logo in the first round of concepts. There's a lot of emotion when it comes to a new brand. It will take time to get that design right. Don't freak out if it's not where it needs to be the first time you see concepts. The right agency should delicately and sensitively walk you through this process confidently.

Find out what's included
Find out how many meetings and refinement iterations are covered within the cost and if there's a policy once you go over. Make them commit to communicating additional costs before they go forward with the work.

The terms
Get a contract: read their terms. Make sure you understand the terms.

Who owns it?
Do you own the finished artwork? If you don't, you may be up for a licensing fee every time you want to print. It's unrealistic to ask agencies to hand over the working files but it's not unrealistic to ensure that you own copyright of the finished product.

Protection is key
Look into trademarking – It offers you the protection you need. Not every designer will have the initiative to suggest this but it is vitally important that the brand you pour your heart and soul into creating is protected.

'Buzz words' don't mean success
Social media is not always the answer! It's a tool. Don't get sucked in to thinking everyone needs a Facebook page, and that it's the answer to your business marketing issues. There's so much to understand about social media before you think it'll have any impact on your business performance and it takes a lot of work, nourishing, interaction and strategic thought. It's worth getting any expert in to help you do this right. Once you have the strategy set, usually someone young should run it (they understand it better than most – it's second nature to them).

Your brand is for the modern era
Engage with a company that understands digital well: It's important that your brand can work well in digital as well as print and you'll find in a lot of cases, the future of your advertising and marketing should have a sizeable digital component. An agency fluent in digital language will ensure your brand is multi-channel and not just appropriate for print.

Have fun
When it comes to branding, have fun. Don't take the process too seriously. It's important, but it doesn't need to be serious. This is supposed to be an enjoyable step forward for your organization and towards success.

**Build
Great
Brands**

Chapter 9

Brand management

Executive Summary

Since writing Build Great Brands, I have received countless positive comments and remarks worldwide and have been privileged to continue the conversation on how we can work together to build great global brands and organizations. This ongoing conversation is exactly what Build Great Brands was designed to generate. Its aim was to not just be a 'Branding 101' but also a guide to understanding the central role that branding has to play in successful growth, both at the startup stage but also further along the journey, when dealing with new growth, products, competition or markets.

When given the opportunity to release a second edition of this book, I wanted to explore in more depth what we as organizations need to do once we have established a great brand. How do we then successfully manage that brand? For this reason I have included a bonus chapter on "brand management" · John

9.1 What is brand management

When we observe the best brands in the world, two things stand out. Firstly, great brands clearly stand for something and they align what they say with how they say it, in a way that cuts through the noise (the noise is the thousands of other messages that bombard us every day).

Secondly, they run deep. They focus on consistently and clearly communicating to the market at every level regularly. Over time this focus has led to the brand creating meaning in the market and standing above the clutter. The returns that companies see as a result of this ongoing investment into their brand are significant. The investment that I am referring to here is not so much about money but about an investment of time and priority. The companies that succeed are the ones that focus their attention on managing the way their brand communicates.

"The best brands in the world stand for something."

9.2 Set the foundation

We must first understand a brand's position in the market, and by position I mean what we stand for, what makes us unique and who we want to be in a market of other brands competing for limited attention. It is our quest to ensure that we position authentically. The positioning exercises contained within this book are of paramount importance to any kind of marketing or advertising because a strong foundation amplifies your voice when communicating to the market. Without proper positioning, we limit our understanding of who we are, what we are trying to say, how we should say it and who our audience is. Our message will not cut through the noise as well as it could. This foundation is what sets us up for success.

But a strong foundation is not enough. It is at best an enlightening and powerful project that engages a company to understand who it is and what it stands for. It is also exciting because, when it's done right, the final brand is a force to be reckoned with. This force is focused and strengthened when the logo, the content and collateral messages, the digital assets, all express the same visual and spoken language. Such co-ordinated focus is the setup that every marketing campaign dreams of having. But it is just the setup. Brand management answers the question 'What next?'

9.3 Drive growth

Building on this strong, authentic foundation requires a strategic approach that captures what matters and drives the marketing, advertising and communication forward in an aligned and driven way.

For this reason, we have developed the brand management framework as a catch-all mechanism to ensure that everything we communicate as a brand is captured, aligned and measured for improvement within one place. It's a full-proof approach to ensuring that a brand is not just looking and speaking well but that it is focused. Brand management strategically plans to reach the short, medium and long-term goals of a business instead of piecemeal, ad hoc, sometimes conflicting and non-measured marketing objects. A great brand management framework must:

1. Articulate the impact a brand has on the performance of the business
2. Have clear goals and KPIs that align with the business performance
3. Capture all communication channels and functions of the business
4. Be easy to understand and execute
5. Keep us aligned and focused on our brand purpose and authentic position as a brand

A brand management framework is more than just marketing. Successful marketing results in lead generation but brand management takes things one step further and looks at the brand experience, the brand culture and the brand reputation of an organization. All these things impact marketing but brand management expands and broadens our focus, to incorporate the other elements within our organization that impact its ability to grow.

9.4 Brand management in a digital age

Brand management is essential in an age of digital branding because the conversation around your company is bigger than it ever has been and the touch points through which to access your brand have increased exponentially. For this reason, it's more difficult to track, control and align every touch point that communicates your brand to the market. Your old Facebook page that was set up way back when hasn't been touched in two years. The voicemail that no one checks is out of date and every client gets sent a newsletter every month with the wrong logo.

Back in the good ol' days it was far easier to manage an audience's experience and perception of your organization because of the limited ways the audience could engage. The message was controllable.

The customer could come visit you or they could call you. If you ran advertising, they may see an advertisement in the paper, but this was about the extent of complexity. Nowadays, we live in a digital age, which provides companies with challenges as well as benefits. In this new age there are many more avenues to talk through and many more ways that your audience can connect with you. Understanding which avenues to pursue and how best to influence or direct the conversation can seem increasingly difficult.

However, successful brand management zooms out and asks the bigger question around who we are and how our audience seeks to engage us and strategically chooses the right channels to set up and manage. Brand management asks the question, 'What do we want to say?' and plans to integrate each channel we utilizeso that we communicate in unison. It forces us to choose to do everything well and perhaps realizethat as fun and 'mandatory' as having a social media presence may be, we may not be able to manage it to the level that will drive us towards our goals.

Consistency is the glue that holds our brand together. We don't do things because they are fun or fashionable but because they best further our strategic goals. There must be a plan around how we talk, what we say and how we plan to connect across our entire digital footprint of which social media is a part. It's exciting when we think big picture because we then find ways to creatively explore what that means for the user experience when they are engaging our brands online. When we learn to integrate all our touch points together in ways that optimizeuser experience, we discover fascinating and valuable new opportunities to build awareness and loyalty.

9.5 The right kind of goals

Brand management ensures that when we run a campaign across one channel, we work to align it with our other active channels and in doing so, amplify its impact. We do this because we've identified our goals and developed strategic approaches to reach those goals. Goals that matter. Not website hits (though this is an interesting metric) but business objectives. Examples of goals that drive the right brand management strategy include:

1. Revenue specific to audience/customer categories
2. Customer acquisition goals
3. Brand awareness / engagement / sign up goals
4. Customer spend measures

It's important that goals always connect to business objectives. When we set goals such as 'grow our database' or 'increase social media engagement', we fail to align branding with business performance. These are indicators and important but important only because they are part of our strategic plan to move towards 'business growth' or 'business stabilisation' based goals.

9.6 No more local

In this digital world, it's important for us to recognize that the age of 'local business' has gone. This isn't meant to tone down the importance of local businesses but the statement is designed to help us realizethat we are actors on a global stage now and our brands must stand up and be noticed on this larger, grander stage. Whether you are intentionally competing globally or not, your audience, even if it is local, is engaging with global brands in your area. This isn't about advertising like Coke or spending the budget of Nike. What it means is that we approach the way we communicate with the same strategic approach as these brands do because this is what our audience now responds to.

"...you have the opportunity to turn heads when you treat yourself like a global brand and commit yourself to doing it well."

People see, interact with and enjoy the brand experience from many brands around the world no matter where they are and they expect the level of quality and strategic thought that these brands exercise from you as well. They are trained, hardwired and conditioned to expect it, and so to consider yourself 'just local' and hold yourself to 'just local' standards is a risk I'd rather you not take. No matter what you do or who you sell to, you have an opportunity to turn heads when you treat yourself like a global brand and commit yourself to doing it well. When we measure ourselves using the local competitors as a yardstick, we set our sights too low. When we imagine ourselves on the global stage and hold ourselves to those standards, we seek to meet and even exceed the expectations our audience has of what it's like to engage with companies like ours. When we think globally, we create an opportunity to do something great and to create brand loyalty, even at the local level. Brands are always on a mission to create loyalty.

9.7 The new marketing approach

We may recognize that we need a marketing plan or a brand plan. We may know that, as business leaders, it is important to have a strategic plan. What tends to happen from there however is that we dream up all the cool things we want to do throughout the year and put it down on paper – and that becomes our marketing plan. We pat ourselves on the back and then wonder how we're going to do it all. Unfortunately, though it may all be on the same piece of paper, the activities are disjointed and unaligned. There isn't enough consideration given to what success looks like and what the plan seeks to achieve over and above an accumulated assortment of projects. It becomes our 'emotional checklist' to help us feel that we're doing what we should. The plan itemises things like, 'engage consumers with social media activity' or, 'run three competitions to our database'. It contains things like, 'do great SEO' or, 'send one mailer to the local area businesses'. These are all great things in themselves but imagine the impact we can have when we start with goals, objectives and three-to-five year visions, which we then leverage to develop a strong strategic plan with metrics in place to get us there.

Brand management helps us put that plan together, strategically, and with goals at the forefront. Then it provides us with the brief to think creatively and track all our activity in one place.

Let me show you how it works and how you can apply it in your business.

9.8 The Brand management framework

We know that a strong brand foundation is important but in order to put our brand to work, we must think about brand management as a planning tool to drive all communication inside and outside of our organizations and to help us grow. We've already invested a great deal of time into determining the authentic values-driven brand position that we know our audiences will engage with. Ensuring that we consistently move forward from that is a challenge and a plan is pivotal.

The brand management framework is designed to capture in one place all the things that communicate us to the market. It's an approach that enables us to take the rights steps in the right order to put together the kind of plan that helps us reach our organizational goals. It is incredibly powerful when used well and provides the structure around which we can insert highly creative ideas.

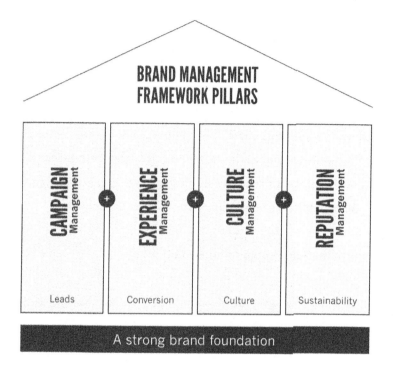

Utilising these four pillars, we develop a toolkit of ideas, projects and assets that drive our planning and strategic thinking and forms a launchpad for creative ideas. This toolkit is always growing and evolving.

1. Campaign management (lead generation)

Too often, campaign management has a short-term focus, designed to generate immediate leads and interest in your organization. But this is only part of the story. Good campaign management requires a strong brand, a strong message and a core idea in order to cut through the noise and to build up a strong presence over time. With a strong

135

foundation and long-term goals in place, it becomes easier to determine which channels to use to reach out to your audience and where and when to spend your money to achieve campaign success.

Few brands choose to continue focusing on results once a campaign is launched. However, this should be the time that measurement is crucial so that we can observe the results to date and make tweaks and changes to channels, spend, time of day, message, colors etc. in order to engage better across the all channels and consumer experiences.

Campaign management is comprised of:

- A channel strategy – online and offline ways to advertise the brand
  i.e. What channels will we use to advertise?
- Messaging and story development – the core idea used
  to communicate
  i.e. What unified idea and voice will we use to drive our message?
- A budget
  i.e. What do we intend to spend, where will we spend it and when?
- A dashboard or record of results
  i.e. How will we measure the results of our lead generation
  activity?
- An optimisation rhythm
  i.e. What experiments will we run and how will the data we find
  help us improve results?

2. Experience management (conversion)

Experience management is one of the most powerful and under-estimated pillars of brand management. It focuses on client interaction and conversion because it recognizes that getting people through the door isn't enough. What matters is the experience that our audience has with our brand at every touch point. Every experience plays a role in conversion, retention and of course advocacy (word-of-mouth endorsement).

You need to establish measurement and review mechanisms in order to continually implement ways to improve the quality of your brand experience. Hands-on exercises designed to help you walk through this process are included in this book. However, learning about experience management is an ongoing journey that must be given discipline and structure to assist in brand management.

Experience management is comprised of:

- Experience mapping (see the relevant chapter in this book) i.e. Where is our experience detrimental to the conversion and loyalty building process?
- Online user journey audits
  i.e. Is our online user journey designed in a way to promote better conversion?
- Review mechanisms to report on experience feedback and improve touch points as needed

i.e. What are we learning from customers?

- Regular rhythms to improve the experience

  i.e. What can we work to improve this quarter to build an even better experience?

3. Culture management (retention)

Culture management builds on the truth that our brand is only as effective as the people that represent it. Although our brand is made up of the printed and digital assets we use to communicate to our audience, it is 100% dependent on the quality and behaviour of the people that represent it each and every day. Investing time into ensuring that the way we speak and embody the brand is consistent is key to any great brand management strategy. All people representing our brand need to buy-in to its values and what it strands for.

Culture management is comprised of:

- Language handbooks

  i.e. How do we speak as an organization consistently? What do we say and what don't we say?
- Careers brands

  i.e. How do attract and engage potential team members with a careers brand that articulates who we are, what we stand for and where we are going?
- On boarding programs

  i.e. How do we initiate new staff to ensure they represent the brand completely?

- Internal communication rhythms

  i.e. How will we plan to communicate with our team on the many projects internally and externally that we are undertaking to grow our organization? How do we engage them internally as intentionally as we do those external to the brand?

4. Reputation management (sustainability)

Every brand requires short-term and long-term goals to maximise effectiveness. Reputation management ensures that our focus and plan are centered on long-term sustainability.

Every brand benefits from looking forward into the next five years in order to put in place strategies now that build for that future. A longer-term view also provides us with a context to evaluate our short-term activities and what part they play in the bigger picture.

A long-term strategy helps build our brand to be a sustainable figurehead in our industry and to live on beyond us. Reputation management builds communities and engages them with exceptional content and communication designed to build stronger brand awareness for the long term. It establishes key media and stakeholder relationships and builds stronger profiles for our brands in the marketplace, working towards brand sustainability.

Reputation management is comprised of:

- Community hub building

  i.e. How do we build a community of engaged people eager to listen and interact with us as a brand?

- Content marketing planning

  i.e. How can we educate the market with content that delivers exceptional value for them?

- Brand profiling in the community, media and industry

  i.e. How will our brand become known as an industry leader and community figurehead for the years to come?

This framework, though simple, provides us with an effective planning tool to build a targeted and intentional strategy. Using it well, however, is dependent on the process required to implement (execute) this planning.

The process

The brand management framework needs to be translated into actions and the following process plan is designed to help you build a strategy that works for the next ninety days, twelve months and five years, simultaneously.

Step One · Identify clear organizational goals

Step Two · Refresh your understanding of the audience

Step Three · Clarify your goals for each pillar

Step Four · Develop a strategy using the tool kit approach to the pillars

Step Five · Think in 90 day stretches

Step Six · Review every 90 days

Step 1 – Identify your organizational goals

What are we trying to achieve in the next one, three and five years. Remember that marketing, communication and advertising are designed to help you achieve your company goals. Step one is to identify clearly what those goals are.

Step 2 – Refresh your understanding of the audience

Revisiting who our audience is, what they value, what they look for and what problem we solve for them is important as it helps us look at our creative ideas through the lens of our audience instead of through our own. When we think like us, then we design marketing and communication plans for us. Brand management forces us to think like our audience and develop ideas through that understanding.

Step 3 – Clarify your goals for each pillar

Each of the pillars will contain a variety of projects, tasks and measures. Before we can even begin to think about what we 'should' be doing, we must set goals for each of the pillars and assign a range of KPIs and measures to define what success looks like.

Step 4 – Develop a strategy using the toolkit approach to the pillars

Start with each pillar and imagine ideas through a toolkit approach. Think about what specific activities could fall under each pillar and use these as brainstorming tools. Begin putting them together as activity plans, all working towards achieving the goals you set for each pillar. Don't include more than you need. Your activity and strategy is purely based on how you will achieve the goals you've set instead of what you think you 'should do'.

Decide if you think each activity is a short-term, once-off project or whether it will continue for the year ahead. Begin mapping a year-long strategy under each pillar, with a range of projects to be undertaken on your road to reaching your goals.

Step 5 – Think in ninety-day stretches

Attempting to fulfil an annual strategy can be daunting and what can happen is that it doesn't get touched for weeks or months. A brand management plan is something you (or someone you delegate) need to be glancing over and acting on weekly. I recommend splitting the annual strategy into ninety-day action plans involving projects, tasks and resources assigned to each task. Creating your ninety-day action plan provides a checklist of tasks to accomplish and measure in easier to digest chunks.

Step 6 – Review every ninety days

The term annual strategy can be misleading, as it seems to suggest that you review it only once a year. This is not the case with the most effective brand management plans. Using our goals as the guide, I recommend embarking on a ninety-day review, where you ask yourself the following questions:

- Did we fulfil all our assigned tasks within our ninety-day action plan? What did we do?
- What did we learn?
- What results did we achieve in relation to our annual KPIs and priorities by pillar?
- What changes will we make to our strategy based on what we've learned?

The value of these reviews is that they allow us to tweak, optimize and shift our strategies and then incorporate them into our next ninety-day action plan. It's at this point that you are welcome to change things as little or as much as you think they need. Your priority is reaching the objectives you set at the beginning of the year. Having them up to date and meaningful is key to driving the right activity, so it's worth readdressing these as well.

The brand management plan is a rolling document that should be reviewed and reset each quarter, whilst ensuring the goals and objectives are always the focus. At different stages in the life cycle of your brand, you will focus on different aspects of the framework. Each pillar is equally important but some will need more attention than others depending on your needs at any given point. For instance, if the organization is preparing to invest in growth, you may drive the focus of activity around the culture pillar, to ensure that your careers and on boarding brand is well aligned. The power of the framework and review mechanism is that it can adjust and flex with the seasons of your business and isn't specific to any one industry.

What now?

A brand management framework gives us the tool we need to stay in control of the way our brands communicate to the market. It asks us to focus on goals first and then activity instead of the other way around. It provides for the long-term and empowers our short-term goals accordingly. It provides the accountability measures we need to ensure that everything is covered for success or otherwise clearly visible, so that strategic adjustments and improvements can be made in real time and in time.

Great brands grow great organizations and in order to do that well, brand management must be at the core of all we do. Employees also respond to strong and effect brand management and become more motivated to achieve strategic goals.

When building a truly great brand, a healthy approach towards auditing and developing a strong brand foundation is the first step, and brand management as a regular discipline within your brand communication is the next.

9.0 Brand management

Build
Great
Brands

Chapter 10

Conclusion

Executive Summary

Time to invest into branding and growth.

10.1 Closing thoughts

It is in the pursuit of a great brand that we better ourselves. That's one of the many things I love about Brand. I also love its incredible ability to keep us on track, to keep us authentic, to keep us focused on our customers and to make us better in everything we do. Brand steers the ship for us.

As you apply the learning, the activities and the actions from this book, I have no doubt that you will find it powerfully aids in the growth of your business.

My message is simple. Let's make the world a better place by building great brands. The more great brands the better. With that in mind, I'll leave you with these three essential aspects to branding. It's important that we continually remind ourselves of these three things and challenge our organizations to improve on each.

1. The Positioning	2. The Strategy	3. The Experience

1. The positioning

Our message and our aesthetic is what will engage our audience either effectively or ineffectively. All the marketing in the world can fall on deaf ears if our message, our positioning and our aesthetic are wrong.

2. The strategy

It must be disciplined, it must be targeted and it must be measured. The right brand plan takes that message to the right people at the right time and in the right way.

3. The experience

We must follow up our message and our strategy with an experience that wins the customer over. We must deliver on our promises and create a series of positive interactions that accumulate in our customers' minds to create a positive impression. It is the taste we leave in our customer's mouth.

And so I wish you all the best as you build your great brand and grow your business. Remember, www.buildgreatbrands.com contains the resources and worksheets within this book.

You are more than welcome to email me at john@jcinquina.com with any stories, comments, questions or general hellos. I'd love to hear from you. John.

www.buildgreatbrands.com

The Author

John Cinquina is no stranger to branding and business growth. As one of the industry's most exciting emerging branding and communications leaders, he has a powerful grasp on what it takes to create and share a powerful message.

Since beginning a brand strategy company fresh out of university, this young entrepreneur built the business into a fast growing agency, providing ongoing brand support for a range of the country's most prominent companies and playing vital roles in helping startups scale quickly to take market share through an exciting and unique brand methodology.

John has been internationally recognized for his success and industry expertise in the B&T 30 under 30 awards, The International Creativity Awards, the International Communicator Awards and the Global Best Brand Awards. His blog on branding was named the best industry blog in Australia by the Australian Web Awards.

Today, John is an active investor and specialist in aligning brand to business strategy. After being awarded a Green Card for his contribution to the field of branding, he works with companies globally from New York City, where he and his family are based.

Notes

Made in the USA
Coppell, TX
10 May 2021

55421317R00085